Make Any
BLOCK
Any Size

Joen Wolfrom

- Easy Drawing Method
- Unlimited Pattern Possibilities
- Sensational Quilt Designs

C&T PUBLISHING INC.

EDITOR: Liz Aneloski

TECHNICAL EDITOR: Joyce Engels Lytle

COPY EDITOR: Vera Tobin

COVER DESIGNER: Christina Jarumay &
BOOK DESIGNER: Micaela Miranda Carr

DESIGN DIRECTOR: Diane Pedersen

ILLUSTRATORS: Joen Wolfrom and Kandy Petersen

PHOTOGRAPHER: Ken Wagner, Wagner Photo Lab,
Seattle, Washington, unless otherwise noted

Published by C&T Publishing, Inc., P.O. Box 1456, Lafayette,
California 94549

Attention Teachers:

C&T Publishing, Inc. encourages you to use this book as a text for teaching. Contact us at 800-284-1114 or www.ctpub.com for more information about the C&T Teachers Program.

Please note: This book contains many original patterns which I have designed. You may photocopy a maximum of two copies each of these original patterns for personal use only. All of my original patterns are protected from any commercial use by international copyright laws. Please contact C&T Publishing for more information. Thank you. J.W.

Wolfrom, Joen

    Make any block any size : easy drawing method, unlimited pattern possibilities, sensational quilt designs / Joen Wolfrom.

        p.   cm.

    Includes bibliographical references and index.

    ISBN 1-57120-068-1 (pbk.)

    1. Patchwork--Patterns.   2. Quilting--Patterns. 3. Patchwork quilts--Design. I. Title.

TT835.W64422 1999

746.46'041--dc21

                        98-37242

                      CIP

Printed in Hong Kong

10 9 8 7 6 5 4 3 2

CONTENTS

Acknowledgments

I have enjoyed working with all who have contributed in some way to the creation of *Make Any Block Any Size*. Those who must be given a very special thanks are Liz Aneloski, Joyce Lytle, Kandy Petersen, and Ken Wagner. They have provided considerable time and talent toward the completion of this book.

As editor, Liz's suggestions and guidance were always welcome. Her talents complemented my own strengths particularly well. Each of us had to make compromises, but in doing so, we believe we have created a book with great value for quiltmakers. As technical editor, Joyce masterfully oversaw the book's technical details. She worked tirelessly, with great adeptness.

My co-illustrator, Kandy Petersen, is like a priceless jewel! Kandy is especially wonderful to work with because she does not attempt to limit my creative ideas. Because she, too, is interested in creating a visually beautiful book, I am able to include a wide variety of illustrations using scores of patterns, colors, and values. This provision for illustrative freedom is unique. I am grateful to Kandy for both her talent and her refreshing creative freedom. She has taken these hundreds of computer-generated illustrations and polished them with her professional finesse.

Ken Wagner is one of the leading quilt photographers in our country. As most of us know, photographing quilts is a difficult task, even for the professional photographer. I believe Ken's knowledge and skill in capturing color, design, and quilting lines on fabric is extraordinary. He has worked hard at perfecting quilt photography. I am extremely pleased to have Ken photograph as many quilts as possible for this book. His care, patience, warm personality, calm manner, and efficiency are appreciated greatly.

I have enjoyed working with Micaela Carr in her effective job as a graphic designer. She was filled with wonderful ideas for bringing this book into practical fruition. I appreciate her generous talents. As always, Diane Pedersen eagerly supported the concepts and visual displays, and made certain everything worked well together. I thank Vera Tobin, also, for her conscientious copyediting. There are many other C&T staff members who have worked diligently to make this book possible. I am thankful for all of their hard work.

I am pleased to include in this book many wonderful traditional quilts for you to enjoy. I wish to thank all of the quilters who so generously shared their work with you and me. Quilting is a great way to make new friends. Over the years I have had the opportunity to meet many wonderful, warm quiltmakers whom I have enjoyed knowing and whose quilts I admire. I am pleased to include a selection of quilts from some of these talented quiltmakers. I know you will enjoy the quilts created by Ellen Anderson, JoAnn Biegel, Jodene Cook, Sarah Dickson, Diane Ebner, Mary Gillis, Lynda Kelley, Harriet Mooney, Narrows Connection Quilt Guild, Audrey Paulsen, Ellen Rosas, Joann Stuebing, Carol Webb, Debbie Wertmann, and Sue Williams.

I wish to thank all of you who have invited me to teach and lecture at your venues since 1984. As well, I must give great thanks to all of you who have taken classes from me, and those of you who have taken the time to attend one of my lectures. I continue to be overwhelmed by your interest, continued support, and friendship. I am filled with gratitude for all you have done for me. You have most surely enriched my life. It is because of you, and for you, that this book has been written.

Fondly,

joen

This book is dedicated

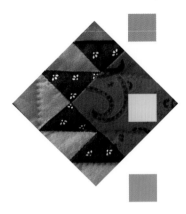

To

Gail Collins,
my sister

who has been such a great friend throughout my life.
Our times together are spent
with lots of laughter, joy, and fun.
I wish her luck in her new phase of life.

To

Larry Barger,
my brother

with whom I have shared work, grand memories, and
innumerable fun-filled adventures.
Alas, I admire his architectural style
with his clean, strong lines,
and unique beautiful designs.
May we continue to enjoy life together.

To

Bruce Barger,
my brother

whose classical music compositions ring beautifully in my ears.
His unbelievable musical talent gives me reason to believe
he could have been a peer to Beethoven, Mozart, or Ravel.
May Bruce have time to compose
all the symphonies, sonatas, and concertos
which are playing in his heart and mind.
His visits, met with great anticipation,
are filled with entertaining spontaneity.

Foreword

Adding To Your Quilting Repertoire . . .

I have written *Make Any Block Any Size* for three important reasons:

First, I want to give you an *up close and personal* view of patch patterns. The patch-pattern families represent both the largest and the most exciting group of quilt patterns in existence today. You could spend your entire quilting life creating quilts just from this wonderful pattern group. An important key to unlocking your own traditional-design potential has much to do with your familiarity with this remarkable pattern collection. If you are able to recognize each family's inner structure and makeup, as well as its strengths and weaknesses, you will be able to make excellent pattern choices before beginning your quilt projects.

Included are over five dozen historic traditional pieced patterns, shown in a lively spectrum of color. Many of the historic patterns included will be familiar to you, while others have rarely been seen. You will find a few dozen original traditional patterns, which I have designed.

All block patterns are shown in full color. Most patterns are shown in a full-view quilt illustration at the end of their respective chapters. This allows you to see the blocks' overall designs. Then you can make good decisions on which blocks to use in your projects.

The second reason for writing this book, and admittedly the most important incentive, is to present you with the easiest method in the world for drawing your own patterns. This procedure involves no math, no calculator, and no fuss. It allows you the freedom to choose any patch pattern and make it precisely the size you wish—even to a fractional number. You can draw any patch pattern easily, quickly, and accurately.

This drawing approach is centuries old. It is truly magical! In our country it has been taught to industrial arts students for decades. Unfortunately, few quilters are aware of its existence. When you learn this age-old magical technique, the doors of opportunity will be open to you. Each pattern chapter goes through step-by-step drawing instructions. The easiest patterns are first in each chapter; the most complex ones are last.

Being able to draw one's own patterns should be part of every quilter's bag of tricks, since it allows you more independence in your pattern selection. If you know how to draw patterns, no longer will you have to wait for a specific block to be published. Nor will you have to search for a much-desired pattern. Instead, you can draw even obscure or rarely published patterns. You may even design your own original block patterns.

Lastly I wrote this book because I am eager to have you witness the fascinating design potential of block blends—the marriage of two blocks. When two blocks are placed together so their interaction creates a new, enhanced design, a successful blend has taken place. Often blended designs are more dynamic and beautiful than solo block patterns. In a chapter of their own, a large selection of block blends are presented for you to peruse. These colorful illustrations show the fantastic design possibilities created when patterns from the same family are joined together. Have a great time experimenting with block blends.

I hope *Make Any Block Any Size* will be a guide and reference for your pattern-drawing skills. If you would like to work further with the concepts presented, the book's last chapter provides activities and extended learning projects for this purpose.

Naturally, I hope this book will bring you many hours of stimulating pleasure. I will be most pleased, if you find many more pattern ideas herein than you have time to sew in the ever-so-near future. Enjoy!

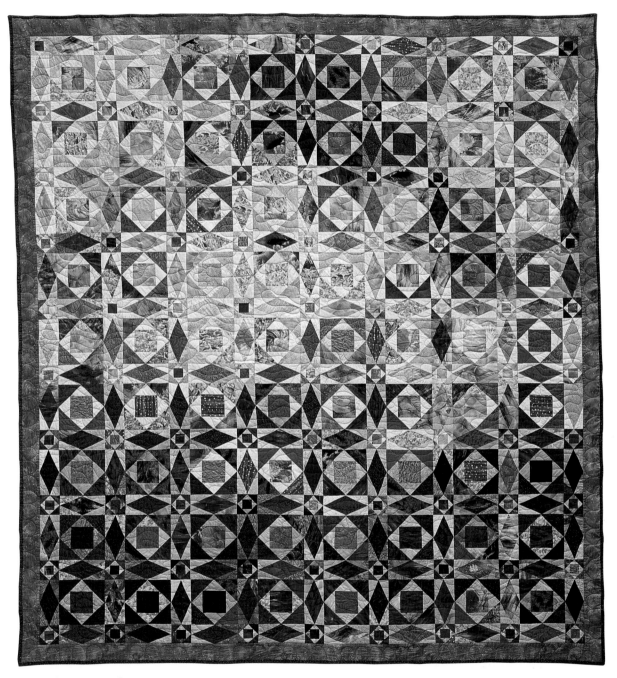

Storm at Sea

Ellyn Rosas, Grants Pass, Oregon
Storm at Sea (four-patch pattern)
Quilt owners: Eric and Barb Rosas
A beautiful array of colors creates a water effect.

Fall's Folly
Debbie Werthmann, Travers City, Michigan
Maple Leaf (nine-patch pattern)
Debbie rotated blocks and added fillers to create
more openness.

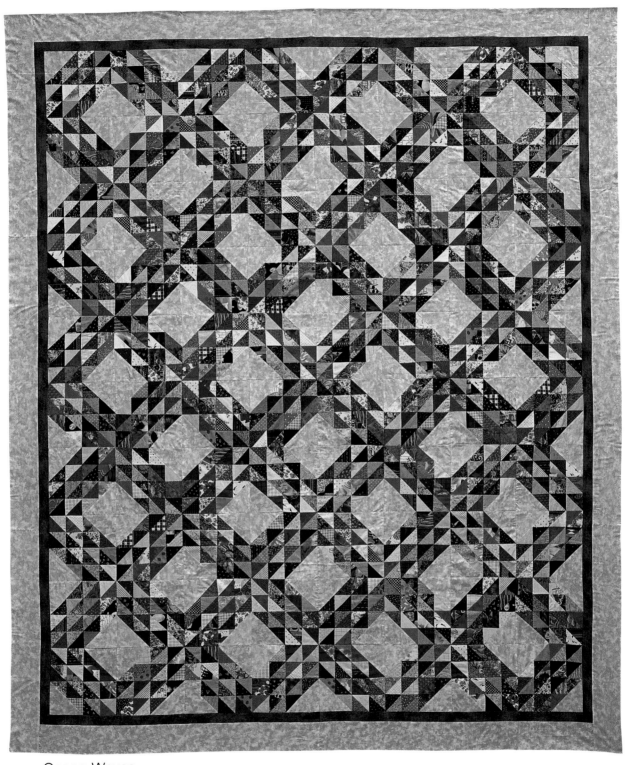

Ocean Waves
Audrey Paulsen, Gig Harbor, Washington
Ocean Waves (four-patch pattern)
Audrey's quilt is beautiful with its wide color and fabric selection.

An Exhibit of Dynamic Traditional Quilts

Spikey and Pete

JoAnn Biegel, Anchorage, Alaska

Nine-Patch Star (nine-patch pattern)

Nine-patch stars are set on-point; the stars vary in color.

Spinning Stars

Lynda Kelley, Tacoma, Washington

Spinning Star (nine-patch pattern)

Dozens of fabrics were used to create this fascinating quilt.

An Exhibit of Dynamic Traditional Quilts

Bear's Paw

Joann Stuebing, Grants Pass, Oregon

Bear's Paw (seven-patch pattern)

Bear's Paw is a scrap quilt with an old-fashioned feeling.

Chapter One
The Patch-Pattern Family Reunion

With thundering pizzazz, the patch-pattern families represent both the largest and the most potentially exciting group of quilts in existence today. This wonderful pattern group brings to us an unlimited array of design possibilities. Without much difficulty, you could spend your entire quilting life creating quilts from this gregarious patch-pattern collection. This wonderful assortment is made up of four-patch, nine-patch, five-patch, and seven-patch patterns. Examples of patterns from each of these families are shown below.

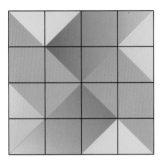

Whirlwind (Four-patch)

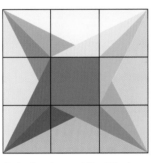

Spinning Around the Block (Nine-patch)

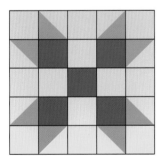

Butterfly at the Crossroad (Five-patch)

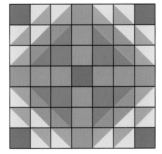

Dove in the Window (Seven-patch)

Most quilters do not take advantage of this great pattern collection's potential, because they do not draw their own patterns. However, if you can draw these patterns, you are free to create whatever your mind wishes—in the exact block size you need. You can use obscure patterns that are rarely published or you can use well-known patterns in the exact size you desire. Also, you are free to create your very own pattern designs. This can be extremely exciting and energizing.

I have written *Make Any Block Any Size* for three main reasons. First, I wish to present to you the easiest pattern drawing method in the world. It involves no math, no calculator, and no fuss. It is magical! You, too, will find it unbelievable in its simplicity.

Secondly, I have selected dozens of historic blocks to whet your appetite and get you excited about using many of these wonderful blocks in your future quilt projects. Each block is shown alone and set in a grid. The majority of blocks are then placed in a quilt setting. This allows you to see a block's overall design potential. I think this is extremely important when selecting a block for a quilt project.

As many of you know, I enjoy making my own block patterns. I have included dozens of these for your enjoyment. I shall be extremely pleased if you select any of these new patterns for your future projects.

Lastly, I am very eager to have you see the wonderful design potential of block blending—bringing two blocks together to form a new, overall design. In Chapter Seven, I have included a large selection of block blends. These colorful illustrations show the beautiful and fascinating design possibilities created when patterns from the same patch-pattern family are put together. I find these blends exciting. I believe they are an important new genre that will explode onto the scene in quilt shows throughout the world in the next few years. Feel free to use any of the block blends I have put together. Also, have fun experimenting with your own block blends. If you want to learn more about block blends, refer to my book *Patchwork Persuasion* (see Suggested Resource Books, page 139).

A Priceless Gift From Our Ancestors— The Secret of Flexible Grids

Only a limited number of patterns are ever published as ready-made block patterns. Even then, the size availability of these patterns is very limited (e.g. 12", 9"). Thus, being able to draw your own patterns allows you great freedom both in design choice and block size. Drawing your own block patterns is fun and easy.

I use a simple, centuries-old, foolproof method to create my own graph paper, so I can draw my block's pattern in the exact size I want. I have used this method for all my patch-pattern quilt projects for over two decades. Every time I teach this method in a quilting class quilters become ecstatic. They are quick to see the unbelievable advantages. Design possibilities unfold before their eyes. As well as the technical benefits of this pattern-drawing method, they are excited about its simplicity and accuracy.

No name seems to be attached to this wonderful drafting method, although it has been handed down through the generations. It simply allows you to make any grid fit any square. It gives you the freedom to customize your grid to meet your pattern's needs. Because of its amazing flexibility, I call it *flexible gridding*.

Flexible gridding has been taught in junior-high drafting classes for decades, but because these types of classes were rarely open to females in earlier years, few of us had the opportunity to learn it—or even to know it was available to learn. Those of us who discovered this drawing method usually did so outside the quilting world. Our teachers were usually draftsmen, architects, or engineers who saw us struggle with pattern drafting and were willing to share their knowledge. My architect brother taught me this method, but my husband learned it in junior-high school. Probably your brother, father, husband, or male friend who had simple drafting or industrial arts training in school remembers this drafting technique. Don't be bashful about asking them for help if you need it.

Flexible gridding is my favorite method of drawing a pattern, because it is simple and gives us the freedom to make any patch-pattern block design to its exact desired size—even to a fraction of an inch. This allows you the freedom to create miniature patterns, medallion centers, or various bed and wall quilts without ever having to buy another published pattern. You can save substantial money by making your own patterns using flexible grids.

I strongly believe flexible gridding should be taught in all basic beginning and intermediate quilting classes. To be able to draw a block pattern is an extremely important skill, because it opens the doors to more freedom in choosing pattern designs and more flexibility in determining the most appropriate block size for the project. During the years I taught basic quiltmaking, students began using flexible grids in their first class. By the end of the session, they could draw any design they wanted in the patch-pattern family.

Flexible grids can be used for every block pattern classified under the four-patch, nine-patch, five-patch, and seven-patch pattern designs. It can be used for other, less familiar, patch patterns too. All patch patterns shown in this book or any other publication can be drawn using this method. Once you know how to use flexible grids, you can create thousands of patterns in any block size.

The Simplicity of Flexible Grids

Flexible grids allow you to easily make custom-made graph paper for your grid. You can duplicate a selected pattern quite easily in whatever block size you choose. To do this, no calculator or complicated math is necessary, only the basics of third-grade arithmetic—skills we all have. The tools are also very simple: white drawing paper, a sharp pencil, an 18"-24" ruler, and a 12" drafting triangle (preferably colored).

The triangle is the only new tool for most of us, and it is easy to use. You can become an expert in less than five minutes. A drafting triangle may be purchased at a quilt store, but more likely you will find it in an office supply store, an art store, or a drafting supply store. Colored triangles are preferrable to clear ones, because clear ones tend to create a glare. Because a triangle is more accurate than a ruler when drawing perpendicular lines and 90° angles, it is a great tool to have.

An Important First Step: Drawing An Accurate Square

Once you determine the block you wish to use, decide what size you want to make this block. The block can be any size. It may be 11", 13", 7¾", 24" or whatever you need for your particular project. After determining your block size, use the following instructions to draw an accurate square. (We will use an 11" block for this particular exercise.)

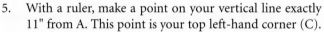

1. To draw the block's bottom line (baseline), place the ruler on the paper near the bottom edge and make finely-made points with a sharp pencil at exactly 0 and 11 on the ruler.

A •————————————• B

2. Draw a line connecting the points. Label the left-hand point A and the right-hand point B.

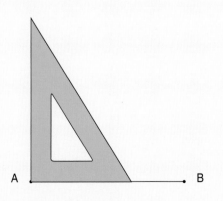

3. Place the bottom of your drafting triangle on the baseline with the 90-degree corner at A.

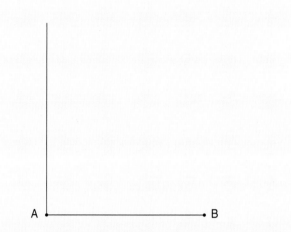

4. Draw a vertical line slightly longer than the 11 inches you need for your block's left side.

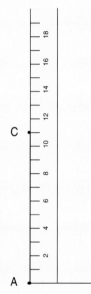

5. With a ruler, make a point on your vertical line exactly 11" from A. This point is your top left-hand corner (C).

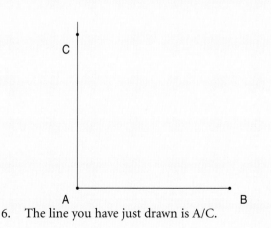

6. The line you have just drawn is A/C.

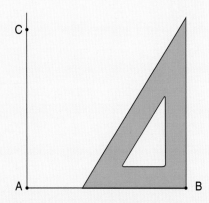

7. With the drafting triangle, draw the block's right vertical side by placing the triangle's bottom 90-degree corner at B.

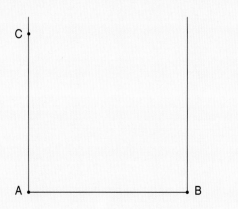

8. Again, draw a vertical line slightly longer than you need.

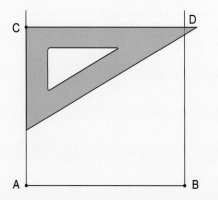

9. Place the triangle on line A/C, so the triangle's 90-degree corner lies precisely at C. Draw a horizontal line. The last corner drawn is D.

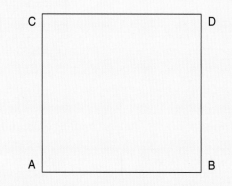

10. The line C/D completes the square.

After the square has been drawn, it is always prudent to check that all four sides are accurate. To do this, place the drafting triangle at each corner. If each corner matches the drafting triangle's 90-degree angle, the square is accurate. If any line is off, correct the problem before going on.

Once you have drawn the block the exact size you wish, you are ready to choose a block pattern and draw the grid lines. You will use the same supplies you used to draw the block: a sharp pencil, an 18"-24" ruler, and a 12" drafting triangle.

Easy instructions are given for each of the patch-families in the following chapters. If you wish to draft a four-patch pattern, go to Chapter Two (page 19) for directions. Chapter Three (page 38) gives specific information about drafting nine-patch patterns; Chapter Four (page 71) gives detailed information about drafting the five-patch patterns. If you have a seven-patch pattern you wish to draft, go directly to Chapter Five (page 86).

Additional Considerations

Choosing Templates Or A Foundation Method

Once your pattern has been drawn, you need to decide whether you will work with templates (plastic or paper), a foundation (paper or fabric), or a combination of templates and a foundation, adding seam allowances where necessary. If you have not made templates before, if you have never experimented with foundation piecing, or if you would like to review either process, refer to one of the many books on the subject (a few are listed in the Suggested Resource Books on page 139).

If you will be making templates rather than using paper or foundation piecing, mark the straight-of-grain lines on each template shape after you have drafted your pattern. Use your drafting triangle for this task. Mark both vertical and horizontal lines. If drawn correctly, these markings will be parallel or perpendicular to the block's perimeter lines.

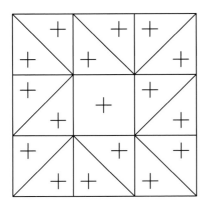

Mark straight-of-grain lines on each template shape.

Your templates should be placed on the fabric so the straight-of-grain markings are either parallel or perpendicular to the fabric's salvage or edge. This extra care in placing the templates on fabric will help eliminate unnecessary stretching and bulging.

Designing Tips

In most designs, your eyes are drawn to the center of the quilt, regardless of the size or design. To create the best design, it is almost always best to use an odd number of blocks horizontally. This allows your eyes to focus on the intended design rather than the background or an obscure part of the design. Because of this design feature, the number of horizontal blocks used is important. The quilt illustrations in this book are shown with odd numbers of horizontal blocks.

Most bed quilts will have three, five, or seven blocks horizontally across the mattress top. Therefore, depending on your project, the block size will vary. To help determine how many blocks will best fit across your bed, see the mattress chart below.

Common Mattress Sizes

crib:	27" x 52"
twin, regular:	39" x 75"
twin, long:	39" x 80"
double, regular:	54" x 75"
double, long:	54" x 80"
queen:	60" x 80"
king, regular:	76" x 80"
king, dual:	78" x 80"

After deciding how many blocks will fit best across the top of your bed, divide the mattress width by the number of proposed horizontal blocks. This answer will determine the block size. After you have determined the size and number of blocks needed to cover the bed top, decide how you will design the bed drops (sides of the bed). Most likely you will combine blocks with a border to extend the quilt's sides. Once your plan is finalized, draw the block pattern to its exact size.

Alas, wall quilts are particularly sensitive to visual balance because they are displayed so clearly. Once you have chosen the block design for your quilt, it is extremely important to find its most pleasing setting. This depends on the pattern(s) you have chosen. To create the best design possible, arrange several paper blocks to determine the most pleasing setting. To learn more about designing your quilts, refer to *The Visual Dance*, Chapter Nine, pages 122-134.

Joyful Play

I hope you find this book filled with patterns you can hardly wait to put into quilts. Be sure to go through the Activities and Extended Learning exercises in Chapter Eight (pages 135-138), so you give yourself the opportunity to learn this book's concepts in a sequential manner. Also, I am particularly excited about having you work with the many block blends provided in Chapter Seven (beginning on page 106). I can hardly wait to see the results of your quilt play. Have a great time!

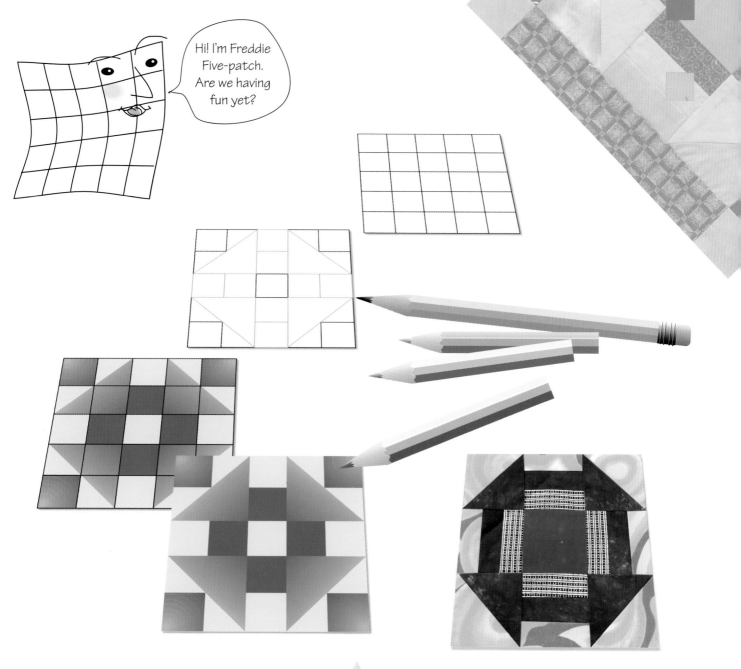

Hi! I'm Freddie Five-patch. Are we having fun yet?

Chapter Two
Flamboyant Four-Patch Patterns

The patterns in the four-patch pattern family are very popular among today's quiltmakers. Only the nine-patch family rivals it in number and popularity. This family is so named because the simplest patterns from this family are made from four squares (patches).

Many well-known patterns belong to this vast group. Four-patch patterns can be divided into three groups: basic, simple, and complex. Basic and simple four-patch patterns are great for beginning quiltmakers, because they are quite easy to construct. As an additional advantage, some of these easy patterns create great optical illusions, especially when blended with other blocks. There are numerous complex patterns, which provide great design opportunities too. Selected quilts from this patch-pattern family can be seen in the photos on pages 7, 9, 59, 60, 62, 64, 66, 67, and 70.

Basic Four-Patch Patterns

(4-Square Grid Patterns)

To create a *basic four-patch pattern*, the block is divided into two equal divisions horizontally and vertically. This creates a four-square grid.

4-Square Grid

Because there are not very many ways to create a design made from a simple four-square grid, the basic four-patch division is a very small group in this pattern family. Birds in the Air, Pinwheel, Windmill, Yankee Puzzle, Streak of Lightning, and Broken Dishes are some of the most well-known of this tiny group. Making Waves is a pattern using triangles in a directional manner in a multiple-block setting.

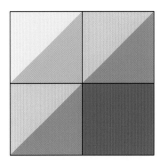
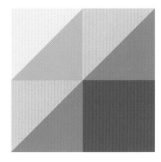

Birds in the Air (Ruth Finley)

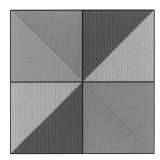

Pinwheel (Famous Features Book Q#5)

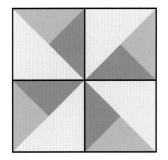
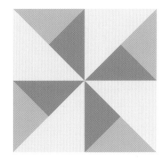

Windmill

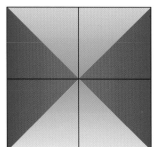
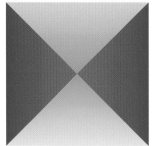

Yankee Puzzle (Ruby McKim)

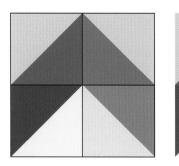

Streak of Lightning

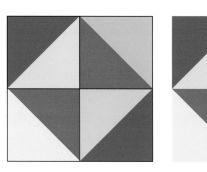

Broken Dishes

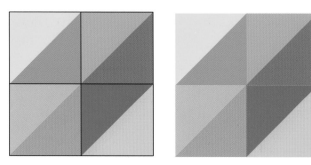

Making Waves (Joen Wolfrom, 1997)

Illustrations showing some of these basic four-patch patterns at work in a quilt setting can be seen on page 32.

Drawing A Basic Four-Patch Pattern (4-Square Grid)

After you have selected the basic four-patch pattern you wish to use, determine its block size. Then draw your block to its exact size (pages 15-16). To create basic four-patch patterns, you will divide your drawn block into four equal squares. To do this accurately, follow the instructions below.

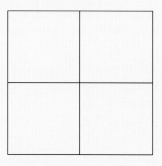

4-Square Grid

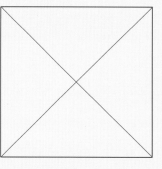

1. Find the mid-point of your block by drawing diagonal lines running from corner to corner. The intersecting point will be the exact middle of the block.

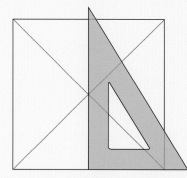

2. Place your drafting triangle next to this mid-point intersection with its bottom edge on your square's baseline. Draw a vertical line from the block's top and bottom perimeter lines, going through the mid-point intersection.

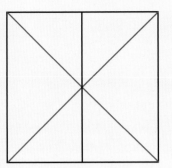

3. After the vertical line is drawn, your square will be divided into two equal divisions.

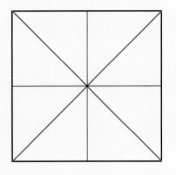

6. Draw a second vertical line.

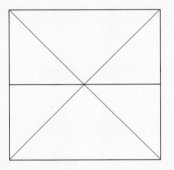

4. After drawing the first vertical line, rotate your block one-quarter turn.

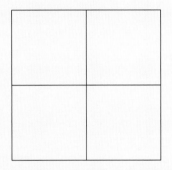

7. These two lines divide the block into four equal parts.

When your four-square grid is drawn, simply draw the pattern lines needed by copying the design lines shown in the pattern. Choose the first line you wish to draw. Continue drawing pattern lines until the entire design has been drawn on your gridded square. For ease and accuracy, use a sharp colored pencil to draw these pattern lines.

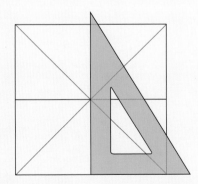

5. Line up the drafting triangle with the square's baseline and intersecting midpoint.

Simple Four-Patch Patterns

(16-Square Grid Patterns)

As you can see, a grid of only four squares does not allow many design options. By dividing the block one step further additional patterns can be drawn. If each block is divided into four equal divisions, horizontally and vertically, a grid of sixteen squares will be created (4 x 4 = 16). Patterns created from this grid are *simple four-patch patterns*.

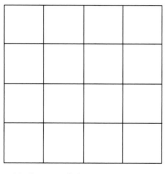

16-Square Grid

There are dozens of simple historic patterns in the four-patch family. I have selected twelve from this vast group. They are Churn Dash; King's X; Flock; Bachelor's Puzzle; Dutchman's Puzzle; Mosaic; No. 18 (Spinning Star); Whirlwind; Yankee Puzzle; Walking Star; Mosaic; No. 6; Star Puzzle; and Balkan Puzzle.

These patterns can be constructed easily, because they are made primarily from squares and half-square triangles. Prior to selecting the block of your choice, meander through the pages showing some of these patterns in their multiple-block settings on pages 32-35, 36 and 37.

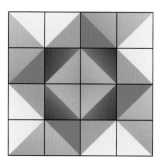
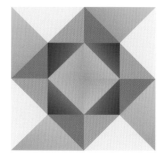

Churn Dash (Ruth Finley)

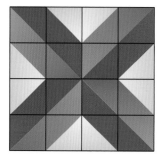
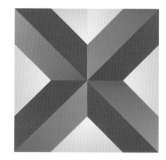

King's X (Farm Journal)

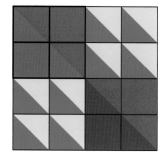
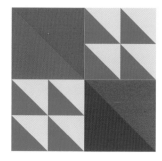

Flock

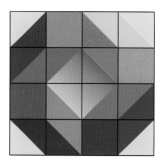
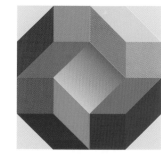

Bachelor's Puzzle (The Kansas City Star, Aug. 8, 1931)

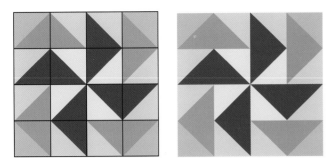

Dutchman's Puzzle (Ladies' Art Company #26, 1889)

Mosaic, No. 18, Spinning Star (Ladies' Art Company, 1898)

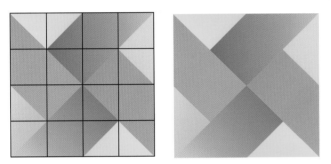

Whirlwind (Ruby McKim: 101 Patchwork Patterns, 1931)

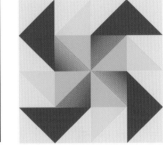

Yankee Puzzle (Ladies' Art Company #28, 1889)

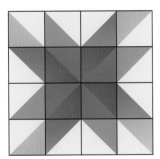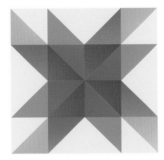

Walking Star

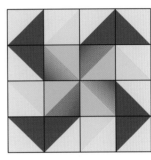

Mosaic, No. 6 (Ladies' Art Company #334, 1897)

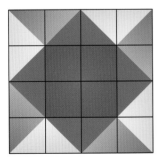

Balkan Puzzle

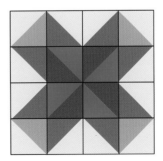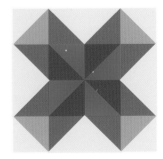

Star Puzzle

Drawing A Simple Four-Patch Pattern (16-Square Grid)

After you have selected the simple four-patch pattern you wish to use, determine its block size. Then draw your block to its exact size (pages 15-16). Once you have drawn an accurate square, look closely at the pattern you have chosen. Count how many equal divisions are needed to create your pattern. A simple four-patch block will need four equal divisions horizontally and vertically.

For learning purposes we will use an 11" block. We need to divide the 11" block into fourths horizontally and vertically.

16-Square Grid

Begin by asking the following questions:

1. What size is my block? . . . . 11"

2. How many equal divisions are needed? 4

3. What number can be divided by 4 and is larger than 11?* 12

   *Note: When determining this, always use the smallest possible number.

4. How many times can 4 be divided into 12? 3

   *Note: The first number (4) is the answer to question #2. The second number (11) is the answer to question #1.

After you have determined the answers to the above questions, you can proceed with the marking of the grid lines. To create simple four-patch patterns, you will divide your drawn block into sixteen equal squares, as shown in the following instructional drawings.

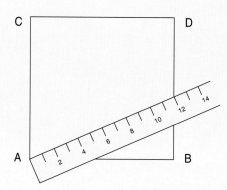

1. With the 11" square in front of you, place the ruler's 0 mark at corner A. The ruler's placement must be exact. Next, place the 12" mark of your ruler on the square's right vertical line B/D (12" is the answer to question #3 listed at left). The 0 ruler marking **must** be exactly at corner A and the 12" ruler marking **must** be on the right-hand vertical line B/D. (If your ruler marking will not fit on line B/D you will need to draw extension lines. See pages 78-81 for detailed instructions.)

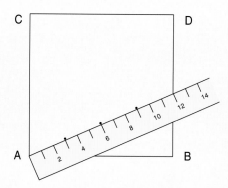

2. With a sharp pencil point, mark every 3" along the ruler edge (12 divided by 4 = 3, the answer to question #4). Make a mark at the 3", 6", and 9" ruler markings.

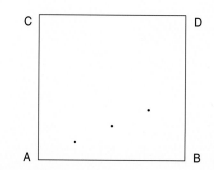

3. The three markings have divided your square into four equal divisions.

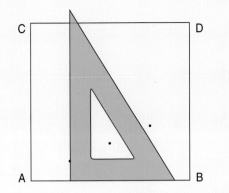

4. Place the triangle on your block's baseline A/B, lining it up to the first mark. Using the baseline and mark as reference points, draw the first grid line. It will be positioned at the 3" ruler marking. Next draw the second grid line at the 6" ruler marking.

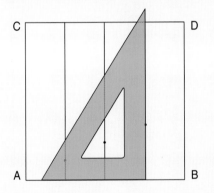

5. Draw the third grid line at the 9" ruler marking. When you draw this line, flip the triangle over, so its bottom edge lies comfortably on the baseline. This allows for better accuracy.

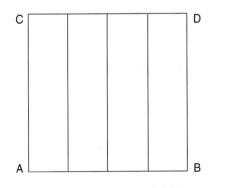

6. You now have your first set of grid lines.

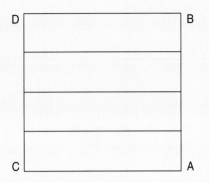

7. Rotate your paper one-quarter turn. Line C/A should be at the bottom of the page, directly in front of you.

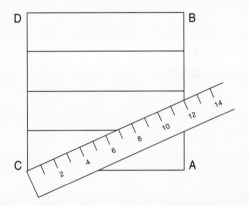

8. Now repeat the earlier steps. Place the ruler's 0 mark at corner C. Place the 12" mark at the right-hand vertical line A/B.

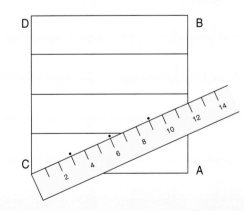

9. Mark every 3" along the ruler, as before. Again, you make pencil marks at the 3", 6", and 9" markings.

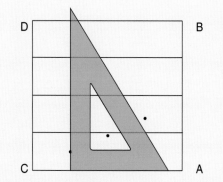

10. With the triangle placed on line C/A and the marks as reference points, draw vertical lines at each marking.

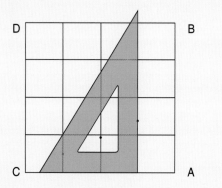

11. Remember to flip the triangle when working on the right side.

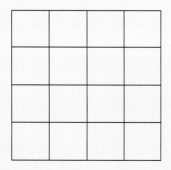

12. You now have a perfect 16-square grid from which to draw your pattern.

Using your selected block as a reference, draw the pattern's design lines, square by square, in your 16-square grid. Use a colored pencil to draw the pattern so the grid and pattern lines do not get mixed up.

Complex Four-Patch Patterns

(64-Square Grid Patterns)

Some of the prettiest and most interesting four-patch patterns need more reference points than the 16-square grid can offer. These *complex four-patch patterns* need to be divided into eight equal divisions, horizontally and vertically. This results in a grid of sixty-four squares (8 x 8 = 64). Thus, patterns made from this grid are considered sixty-four square grid patterns. Naturally, not every grid line or intersecting point will be needed to draw the pattern.

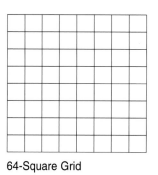

64-Square Grid

Because the number of patterns is so plentiful in this complex four-patch family, it was difficult to choose a pattern selection to represent this membership. I have included a few well-known patterns, such as Delectable Mountains, Blackford's Beauty, and Storm at Sea, along with more obscure designs like Nancy's Fancy, Rolling Star, Laurel Wreath, Dutch Rose, and Stepping Stones. I hope you will enjoy these eight historic patterns.

Over the years I have designed many complex four-patch patterns. I have selected eight for you to include in your pattern library. One pattern, Celebration, was made as a tribute to our Fourth of July celebration. The other patterns are Illusionary Star, Framed Star, Woven Star, Star Lattice, Echoes, Fleeting Star, and Fly Away. As you can tell, I really like stars!

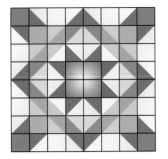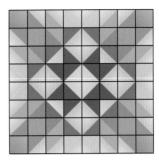

Nancy's Fancy

Delectable Mountains

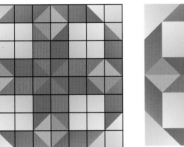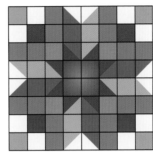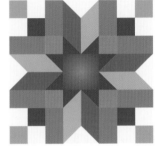

Rolling Star (Ladies' Art Company #4, 1889)

Blackford's Beauty (Ladies' Art Company, #388)

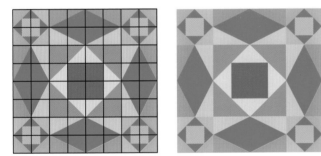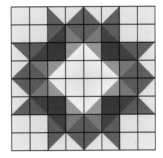

Storm at Sea (Ladies' Art Company, #135, 1895)

Laurel Wreath

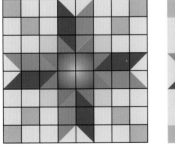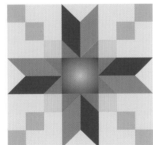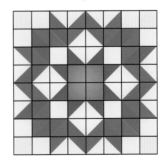

Stepping Stones (The Kansas City Star, 1931)

Dutch Rose (Ladies' Art Company, #185, 1895)

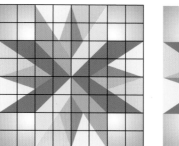 

Illusionary Star (Joen Wolfrom, 1996)

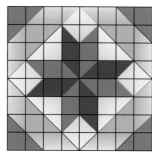 

Framed Star (Joen Wolfrom, 1997)

Woven Star (Joen Wolfrom, 1997)

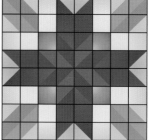 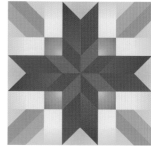

Star Lattice (Joen Wolfrom, 1996)

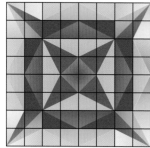 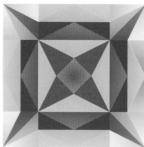

Echoes (Joen Wolfrom, 1998)

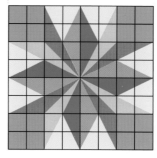 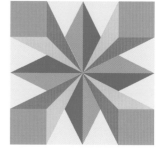

Celebration (Joen Wolfrom, 1995)

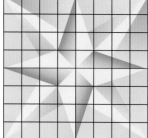 

Fleeting Star (Joen Wolfrom, 1997)

 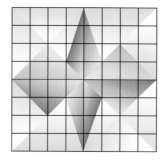 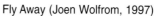 

Fly Away (Joen Wolfrom, 1997)

Drawing A Complex Four-Patch Pattern (64-Square Grid)

If you would like to create a quilt using a complex four-patch pattern, use the following instructions. First, determine your block size and the pattern you wish to use. Draw the square to its exact size (pages 15-16). All complex four-patch patterns need a grid made from eight equal divisions horizontally and vertically.

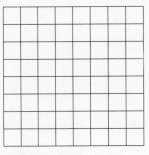

64-Square Grid

For learning purposes we will use a 7" block. To begin, we ask ourselves the following questions:

1. What size is my block? . . . . 7"

2. How many equal divisions are needed? 8

3. What number is larger than the block size, and can be divided by 8?* 8

   *Note: When determining this, always use the smallest possible number.

4. How many times does 8 go into 8? 1

After you have determined the answers to the above questions, proceed with the marking of the grid lines. To create complex four-patch patterns, you will divide your drawn block into eight equal divisions horizontally and vertically.

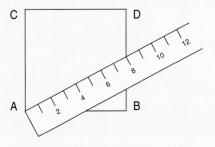

1. With a 7" block in front of you, place the ruler's 0 mark at corner A. The ruler's placement must be exact. Next, place the 8" mark of your ruler on the square's right vertical line B/D. (8" is the answer to question #3 listed on the left.) (If your ruler marking will not fit on line B/D, you will need to draw an extension line. See pages 78-81 for detailed instructions.)

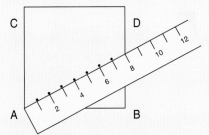

2. Mark a sharp point every 1" along the ruler edge (8 divided by 8 = 1; the answer to question #4).

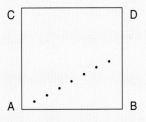

3. Your markings will divide the square into eight equal divisions.

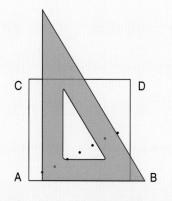

4. Place the triangle on your block's baseline A/B, lining it up to the first mark. Using the baseline and mark as reference points, draw the first grid line. Continue drawing the vertical grid lines, using the drafting triangle.

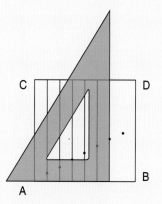

5. As you work on the right side of your block, flip the triangle over, so the 90-degree angle is on the right side of the square.

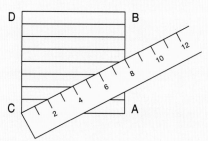

6. You have now drawn the first set of grid lines.

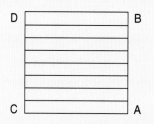

7. Rotate your paper one-quarter turn. Line C/A should now be at the bottom of the page, directly in front of you.

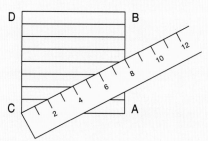

8. Now repeat the same process as done previously. Place the ruler's 0 mark at corner C and the 8" mark at the right-hand vertical line A/B.

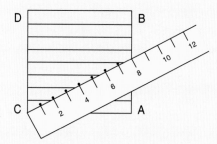

9. Mark every 1" along the ruler.

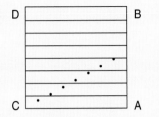

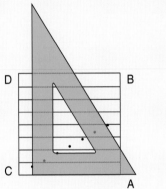

10. When these markings have been made, the square will be divided into 8 equal parts.

11. With the triangle placed on line C/A and using the marks as reference points, draw vertical lines at each marking.

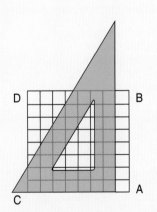

12. As you work on the right side of your block, flip the triangle over, so the 90-degree angle is on the right side of the square.

13. You now have a perfect 64-square grid from which to draw your pattern.

With your pattern in front of you, draw its design lines in your gridded block's square.

Multiple Block Quilt Settings

It is important to see how a block interacts in a multiple-block setting before beginning a quilt project. Some four-patch patterns are shown in quilt settings on the following pages. Make your own paper-block quilt if your selected pattern is not shown in a quilt setting.

Four-Patch Pattern Quilts

Birds in the Air

Streak of Lightning

Yankee Puzzle

Flock

Mosaic, No. 6

Whirlwind

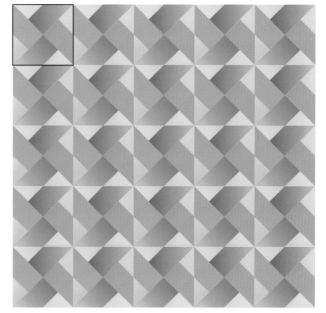

Bachelor's Puzzle

Yankee Puzzle

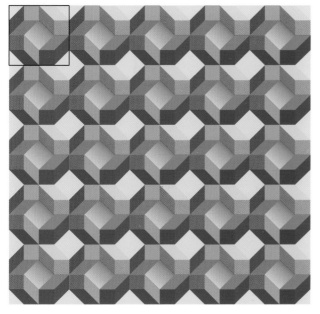

Flamboyant Four-Patch Patterns

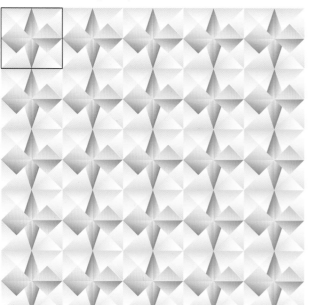

Fly Away

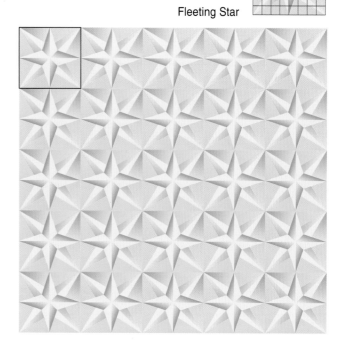

Fleeting Star

Storm at Sea

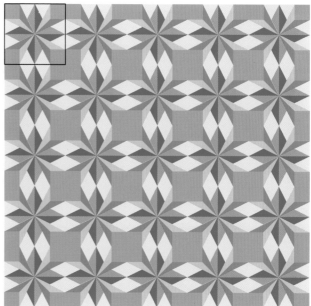

Celebration

Illusionary Star

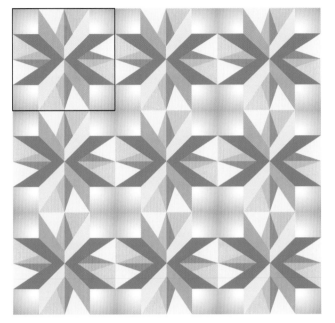

Framed Star

Churn Dash

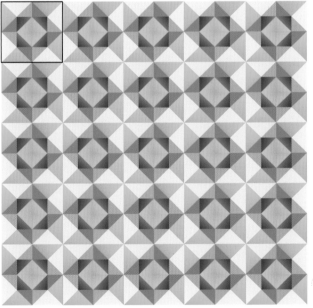

Stepping Stones

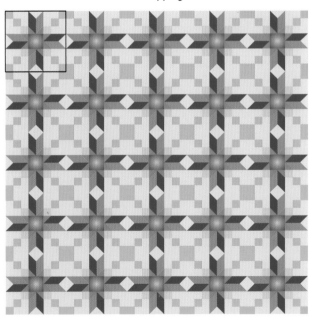

Flamboyant Four-Patch Patterns

King's X

Woven Star

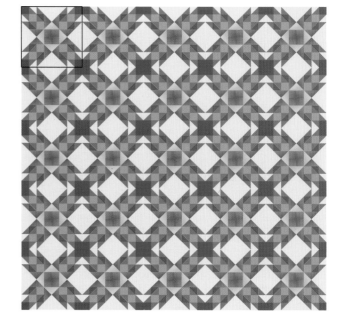

Echoes

Rolling Star

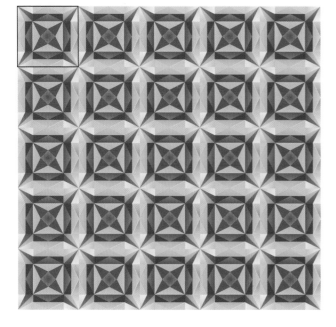

Make Any Block Any Size

Delectable Mountains

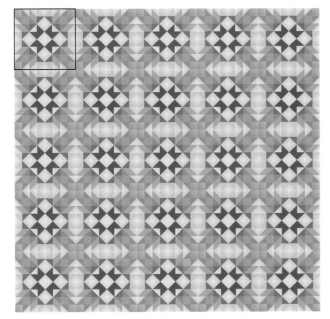

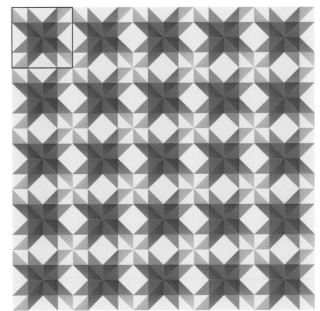

Blackford's Beauty

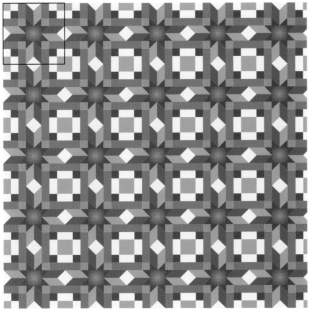

Nancy's Fancy

Flamboyant Four-Patch Patterns

Chapter Three

Nifty Nine-Patch Patterns

The nine-patch pattern family is one of the most popular pattern collections known to quilters. If you substitute the word square for the word patch, you can easily understand how this pattern family was named. Every nine-patch pattern begins as a block divided into three equal divisions horizontally and vertically. When these divisions are made, nine squares or patches appear in the block (see illustration below).

Nine-patch patterns can be divided into three groups, depending on their degree of difficulty: basic, simple, and complex. Each group is described and illustrated in the following pages. Some of my favorite historic nine-patch patterns are included here. A few will be quite familiar to you while others will be less known. Also, I have included nine patterns, which I have designed.

Basic Nine-Patch Patterns

(9-Square Grid Patterns)

The simplest nine-patch patterns need only the basic nine-square grid to create their designs. These are called *basic nine-patch patterns*. These patterns only need three equal divisions, horizontally and vertically, to create their designs (3 x 3 = 9-square grid). Once the grid is made, a pattern's shapes can be drawn using the grid lines and their intersecting points.

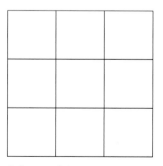

9-Square Grid

Often basic nine-patch patterns are used for beginning projects. Historic examples include Shoofly, Spinning Star, North Wind (also known as Corn and Beans), and Formal Garden. Two easy blocks, which I have designed, are Spinning Around the Block and Gift Box. They, too, only need a basic nine-patch grid. However, diagonal lines from the corners are used in each of these patterns to complete the design.

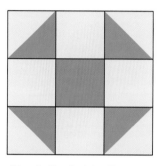 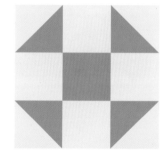

Shoofly (Ladies' Art Company, #276, 1897)

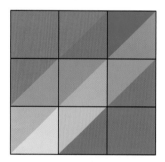 

Northwind (Delores Hinson); Corn and Beans (Hearth and Home)

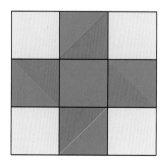 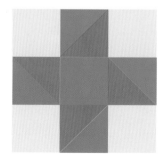

Spinning Star

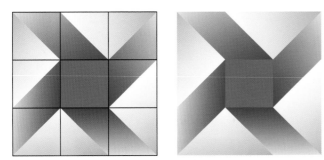

Formal Garden (Farm Journal)

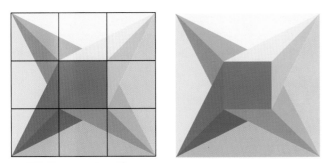

Spinning Around the Block (Joen Wolfrom, 1997)

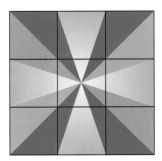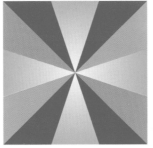

Gift Box (Joen Wolfrom, 1997)

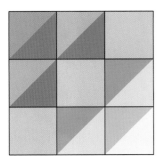

Double X, #1

These easy patterns are used often in quilts because their simplicity allows for quick piecing. The historic patterns Shoofly and Spinning Star are two such patterns. A few simple nine-patch patterns are blessed with strong, graphic design potential. Formal Garden is an excellent example. Its few pattern pieces can create a design that reverberates with color and value changes. Since I enjoy strong graphic design, I am pleased with the visual results of both Spinning Around the Block and Gift Box when they are placed in a multiple-block setting (pages 50-51). Indeed, the overall designs look much more complicated than they are.

Most traditional patterns are symmetrical. Each half or quarter of the pattern is a mirror-image of its opposite side. There is no need to rotate a symmetrical pattern, as no design change takes place. You will find a few asymmetrical block patterns in our historical archives. Unlike symmetrical blocks, these patterns may be used to create additional design options. When an asymmetrical design is rotated, it creates added interest. Several nine-patch patterns are asymmetrical. Northwind allows for interesting pattern play because of its asymmetry. One illustration on page 50 shows Northwind in its traditional block setting. A new design evolves when every other block is rotated a quarter turn (page 50). The difference between these two examples is quite noticeable. It appears as if two different patterns were used. Consider rotating the blocks of any asymmetrical patterns.

If you would like to use any of the above-mentioned basic nine-patch patterns in your quilt project, follow the easy instructions, beginning on page 40, for drawing your pattern. Also, use these instructions to draw any basic nine-patch patterns you wish to use, including those found in other publications.

Nifty Nine-Patch Patterns

Drawing A Basic Nine-Patch Pattern (9-Square Grid)

First determine the block size you need, and then draw it (page 15-16). Once you have drawn the square, look closely at the block pattern you have chosen. Count how many horizontal divisions are needed to create your pattern. A basic nine-patch block will need three equal divisions horizontally and vertically.

9-Square Grid

For the learning exercise, the pattern will be drafted in an 8" block. We need to divide the 8" block into thirds. This can be done easily using flexible gridding. We begin by asking ourselves the following simple questions:

1. What size is my block? . . . . 8"

2. How many equal divisions are needed? 3

3. What number can be divided by 3 and is larger than the block size? 9

   Note: When determining this, always use the smallest possible number. For example, with an 8" block, if you want 3 equal divisions, choose 9 instead of 12 or 15.

4. How many times does 3 go into 9? 3

After you have determined the answers to the above questions, proceed with the marking of the grid lines. To create any of these basic nine-patch patterns, you will divide your drawn block into nine equal sections, using the following instructions.

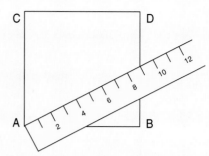

1. With the 8" square in front of you, place the ruler's 0 mark at corner A. The ruler's placement must be exact. Next, place the 9" mark of your ruler on the square's right vertical line B/D (9 is the answer to question #3 listed on the left). Make certain your 0 ruler marking is exactly at corner A and the 9" ruler marking is on the right-hand vertical line B/D.

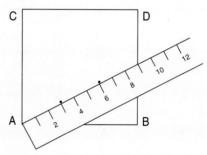

2. With a sharp pencil point, mark every 3" along the ruler edge (9 divided by 3 = 3, the answer to #4). Mark at the 3" and 6" ruler markings.

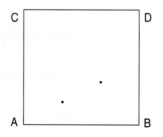

3. These two marks will divide your block into three equal divisions.

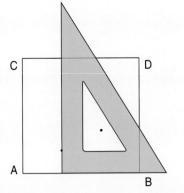

4. Place the drafting triangle on your block's baseline A/B, lining up the triangle to the first mark. Using the baseline and mark as reference points, draw the first grid line.

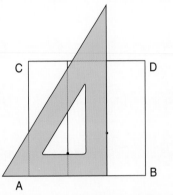

5. Next draw the second grid line at the 6" ruler marking. Flip the drafting triangle, so the 90-degree angle is on the right side.

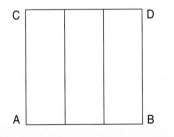

6. Now, your square has been divided into three equal vertical divisions.

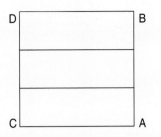

7. Rotate your paper one-quarter turn. Line C/A should now be at the bottom of the page, directly in front of you.

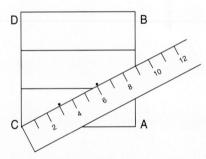

8. Now repeat the same process as previously shown. Place the ruler's 0 mark at corner C. Place the ruler's 9" mark at the right-hand vertical line A/B. Mark every 3" along the ruler, as you have done previously. You will mark at the 3" and 6" markings.

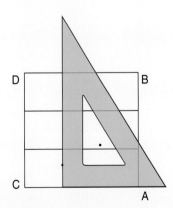

9. Place the drafting triangle on baseline C/A and the first mark. Draw the first vertical line.

Nifty Nine-Patch Patterns

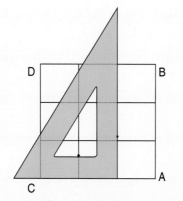

10. Flip your triangle so its 90-degree angle is on the right. Line it up with baseline C/A and the second marking. Draw the next vertical line.

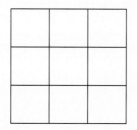

11. You now have a perfect nine-square grid from which to draft your pattern.

With your pattern in front of you, draw its design lines, square by square. Use a colored pencil to draw the pattern so the grid and pattern lines do not get mixed up.

The Nine-Patch Mainstay— Simple Nine-Patch Patterns

(36-Square Grid Patterns)

Simple nine-patch patterns are used by the majority of quiltmakers. Most nine-patch patterns belong to this group. These patterns need six equal divisions horizontally and vertically in order to create their designs. This results in a grid of thirty-six squares (6 divisions x 6 divisions = 36-square grid) These grid lines offer more design capabilities than the simple nine-patch grid. Generally, these patterns are quite easy to construct.

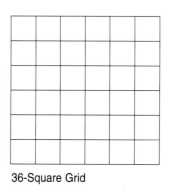

36-Square Grid

Designs that fit into this thirty-six-square-grid category are numerous. I have chosen a few historic patterns from this large group. Most of us are familiar with Fifty-four-Forty or Fight and Dublin Steps but many of us do not recognize the charming Storm at Sea, Wyoming Valley, Weathervane, or Summer Winds patterns. Six new patterns I have designed are also members of the simple nine-patch group. They are Diamond in the Rough, Star Flower, Dancing Star, Star Walk, Wedding Ring Glow, and Puzzling Star.

Weathervane may be placed in either the simple or complex nine-patch groups. If you want to use a 36-square (simple) grid, you will need to break up eight of the gridded squares to create the smaller squares and triangles by drawing diagonal lines from corner to corner, and then drawing the appropriate lines in these squares. For detailed directions see pages 20-21.

Puzzling Star and Dancing Star may be defined more easily by using a ruler's edge to help clarify the connecting lines and intersecting points.

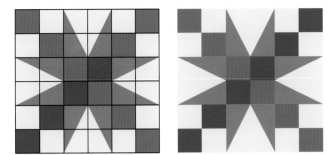

Fifty-four-Forty or Fight Variation (Ruth Finley)

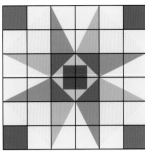 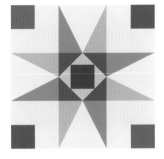

Storm at Sea

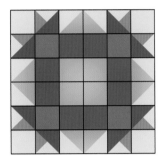 

Weathervane

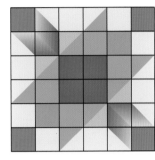 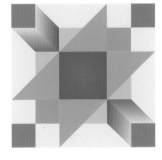

Dublin Steps

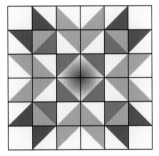 

Wyoming Valley (Nancy Cabot)

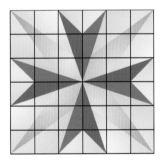 

Dancing Star (Joen Wolfrom, 1996)

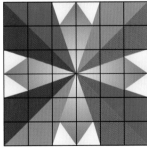 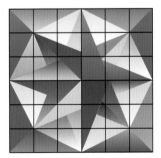

Diamond in the Rough (Joen Wolfrom, 1998)

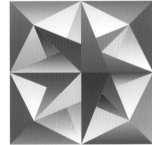

Puzzling Star (Joen Wolfrom, 1994)

Nifty Nine-Patch Patterns

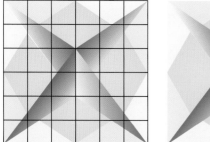

Star Walk (Joen Wolfrom, 1996)

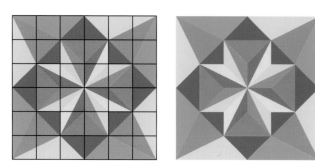

Wedding Ring Glow (Joen Wolfrom, 1994)

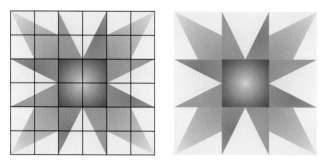

Star Flower (Joen Wolfrom, 1996)

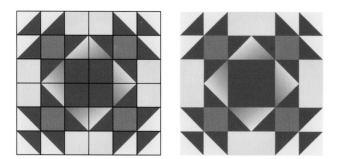

Summer Winds (Nancy Page) Variation (Joen Wolfrom)

Drawing A Simple Nine-Patch Pattern (36-Square Grid)

To create a quilt using one of the simple nine-patch patterns, determine the block size and select the pattern to be used. Draw the square to its exact size (pages 15-16). All simple nine-patch patterns need a grid made from six equal divisions horizontally and vertically.

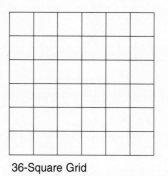

36-Square Grid

For learning purposes we will use a 10" block. To begin, we ask ourselves the following questions:

1. What size is my block? . . . . 10"

2. How many equal divisions are needed? 6

3. What number is larger than 10 and can be divided by 6?* (6 is the answer to question #2) 12

   *Note: When determining this, always use the smallest possible number.

4. How many times does 6 go into 12? 2

After you have determined the answers to the above questions, proceed with the marking of the grid lines. To create these simple nine-patch patterns, you will divide your drawn block into thirty-six equal squares.

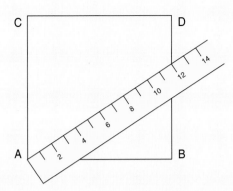

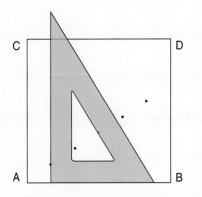

1. With a 10" block in front of you, place the ruler's 0 mark at corner A. The ruler's placement must be exact. Next place the 12" (answer to #3 on page 44) mark of your ruler on the square's right line B/D before proceeding to the next step. (If your ruler marking will not fit on line B/D you will need to draw extension lines. See pages 78-81 for detailed instructions.)

4. Place the drafting triangle on your block's baseline A/B, lining it up with the first mark. Using the baseline and dot as guides, draw the first grid line.

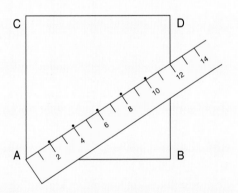

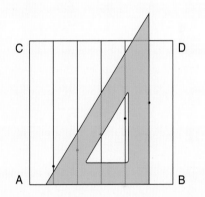

2. Mark a sharp point every 2" along the ruler edge (12 divided by 6 = 2, the answer to #4 on page 44). In this example, you will make a mark at the 2", 4", 6", 8", and 10" ruler markings.

5. Continue drawing the vertical grid lines, using the drafting triangle. As you work toward the right side of your block, flip the triangle over, so the 90-degree angle is on the block's right side.

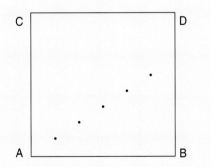

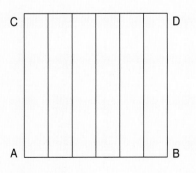

3. These markings divide your block into six equal divisions.

6. When you have completed this step, you will have drawn the first set of grid lines.

Nifty Nine-Patch Patterns

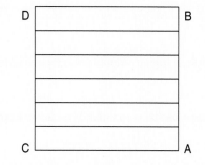

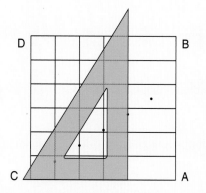

7. Rotate your paper one-quarter turn. Line C/A should now be at the bottom of the page, directly in front of you.

10. As you work toward the right side of your block, flip the triangle over, so the 90-degree angle is on the block's right side.

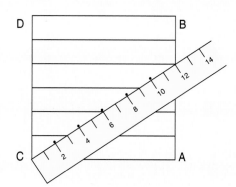

8. Now repeat the same process as previously shown. Place the ruler's 0 mark at corner C. Place the 12" mark at the right-hand vertical line A/B. Mark every 2" along the ruler, as before.

11. When you have drawn the second set of vertical lines, you will have a perfect 36-square grid.

With your pattern in front of you, draw its design lines within your block's grid. Use a sharp colored pencil to draw the pattern lines.

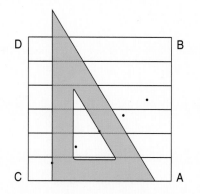

9. With the drafting triangle placed on line C/A and lined up next to the first marking, draw the first vertical line. Continue drawing the vertical grid lines, using the drafting triangle.

Complex Nine-Patch Patterns

(144-Square Grid Patterns)

Complex nine-patch patterns are the most intricate designs in this family. These patterns need twelve equal divisions horizontally and vertically. This division results in a 144-square grid (12 x 12 = 144 square grid).

Few historic nine-patch patterns are members of this complex group. Vermont and Blazing Star are examples of this small, diverse group of elite patterns. Over the years I have enjoyed creating complex nine-patch patterns. Star Echoes is one of these patterns.

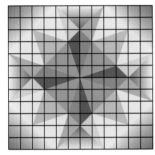

Vermont (Hearth and Home)

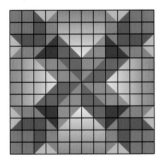
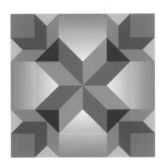

Blazing Star (The Kansas City Star, 1930)

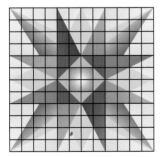

Star Echoes (Joen Wolfrom, 1997)

Drawing A Complex Nine-Patch Pattern (144-Square Grid)

Begin by determining your block's size and the pattern you wish to use. Draw the square to its exact size (pages 15-16). All complex nine-patch patterns need a grid made from twelve equal divisions horizontally and vertically.

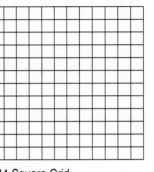

144-Square Grid

For learning purposes we will use an 11" block. To begin, we ask ourselves the following questions:

1. What size is my block? . . . . 11"

2. How many equal divisions do I need in order to draw my pattern? 12

3. What number is larger than my block size and can be divided evenly by 12?* 12

    *Note: When determining this, always use the smallest possible number.

4. How many times does 12 go into 12? 1

After you have determined the answers to the above questions, proceed with making the grid lines for your complex nine-patch pattern.

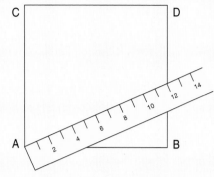

1. With the 11" block in front of you, place the ruler's 0 mark at corner A. Next place the 12" (answer to #3 on page 47) mark of your ruler on the square's right vertical line B/D. (If your ruler marking will not fit on line B/D you will need to draw extension lines. See pages 78-81 for detailed instructions.)

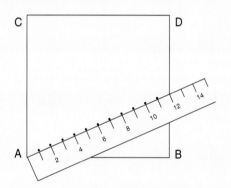

2. Mark every 1" along the ruler's edge (12 divided by 12 = 1, the answer to #4 on page 47). In this example, you will make a mark at the 1", 2", 3", 4", 5", 6", 7", 8", 9", 10", and 11" ruler markings.

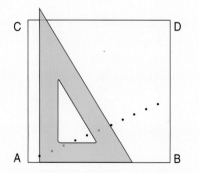

3. Using the baseline and first mark (1") as reference points, draw the first grid line with the triangle. Continue drawing the vertical grid lines, using the drafting triangle.

4. Flip the drafting triangle when drawing the vertical lines on the right side of the square.

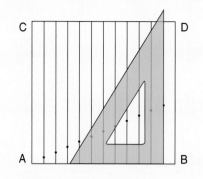

5. When all vertical lines are drawn, you have completed your first set of grid lines.

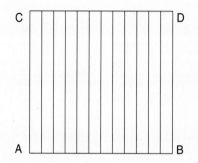

6. Rotate your paper one-quarter turn. Line C/A should be at the bottom of the page, directly in front of you.

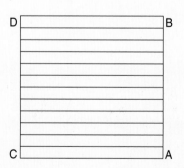

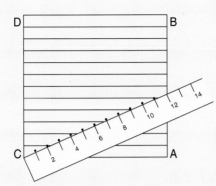

7. Place the ruler's 0 mark at C. Place the 12" mark at the right-hand vertical line A/B. Mark every 1" along the ruler, as previously done.

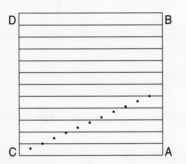

8. With these markings, your block will be divided into a second set of twelve equal divisions.

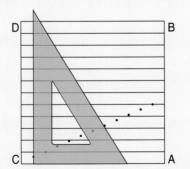

9. With the drafting triangle placed on line C/A and using the dots as reference points, draw vertical lines at each marking.

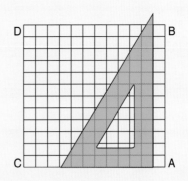

10. As you move toward the right side of the square, flip the drafting triangle, so its 90-degree angle is on the square's right side.

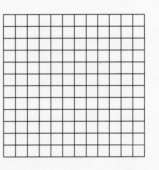

11. When you have completed drawing this second set of lines, you will have a perfect 144-square grid.

With your pattern in front of you, draw its design lines in your block's gridded square. Use a sharp colored pencil to draw your pattern lines.

Multiple Block Quilt Settings

It is very important to know what a selected block looks like when multiple blocks are placed in an over-all quilt design. Therefore, beginning on the next page several blocks are shown in an overall quilt design.

Nifty Nine-Patch Patterns

Formal Garden

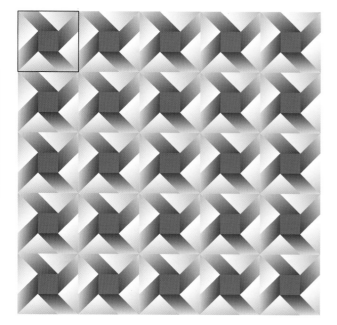

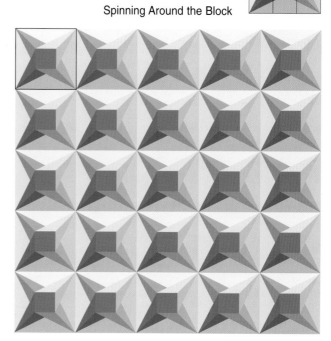

Spinning Around the Block

Northwind, Corn and Beans:
Traditional Setting

Northwind, Corn and Beans:
Setting Variation

Make Any Block Any Size

Gift Box

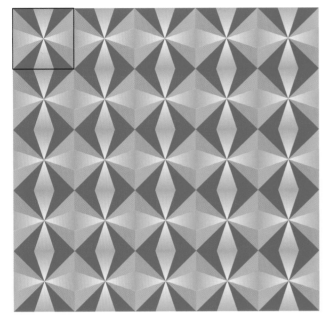

Dancing Star

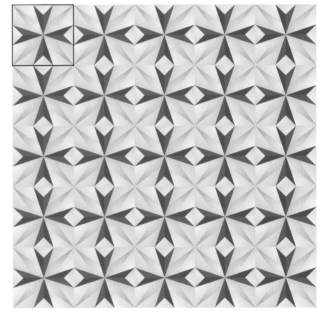

Vermont

Diamond in the Rough

Nifty Nine-Patch Patterns

Storm at Sea

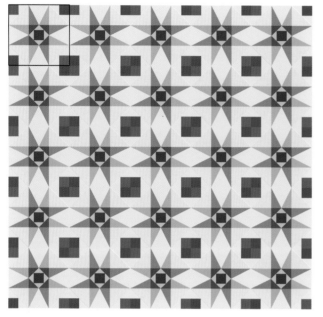

Wyoming Valley

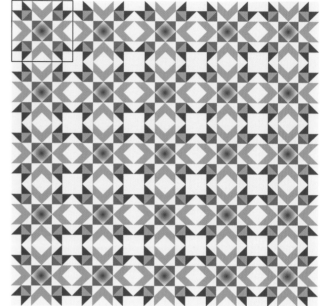

Puzzling Star

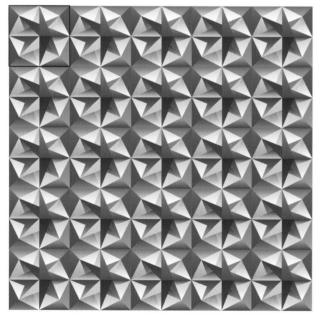

Fifty-four-Forty or Fight:
Setting Variation

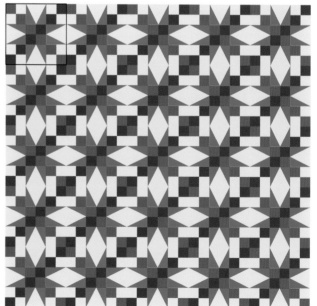

Summer Winds

Star Echoes

Star Walk

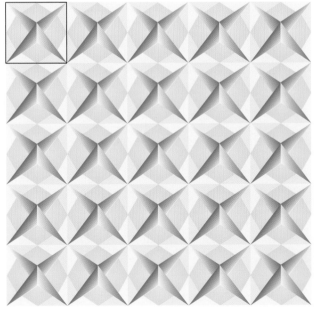

Blazing Star

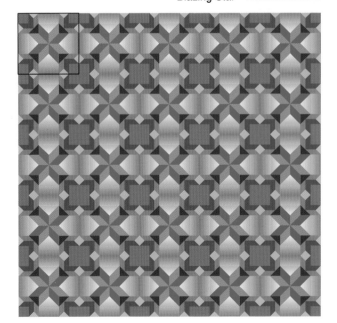

Nifty Nine-Patch Patterns

Love in Fall; Fall in Love

JoAnn Biegel, Anchorage, Alaska

Mosaic, No. 21 Variation (four-patch pattern)

The on-point square border relates very well to the pieced inner design. This design
was inspired by Martha Thompson's quilt *Autumn Romance* (QNM, November, 1993).

Fractured Plains
Lynda Kelley, Tacoma, Washington
Nine-Patch Variation (nine-patch pattern)
Fractured Plains uses a beautiful display of values
and hues to create a play of light.

An Exhibit of Beautiful Traditional Quilts

Noah's Ark

Sue Williams, Gig Harbor, Washington
Shoofly (nine-patch pattern)
Sue made this memory quilt for a family member.

Teddy Bear's Picnic
JoAnn Biegel, Anchorage, Alaska
Bear's Paw (seven-patch pattern)
This is a beautiful scrap quilt using plaids.

An Exhibit of Beautiful Traditional Quilts

Stars of Seabeck

Sue Williams, Gig Harbor, Washington

Fifty-four-Forty or Fight Variation (nine-patch pattern)

Sue combined this block with an elongated triangle to create the graceful illusionary curves. This quilt has been hand stippled.

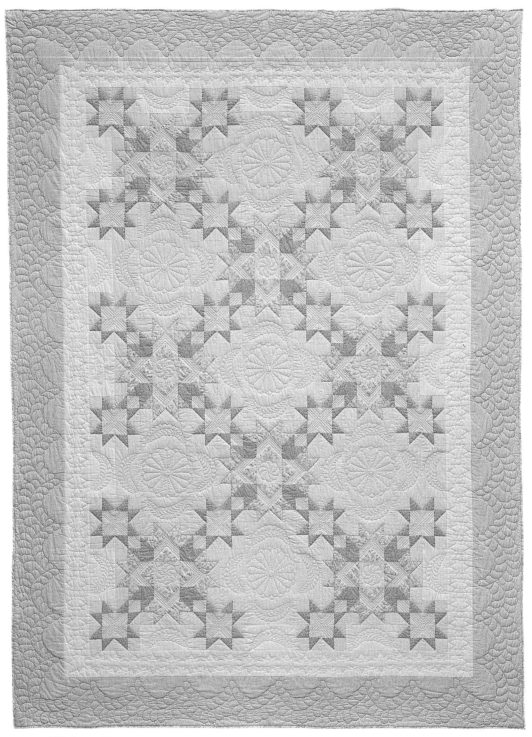

Ribbon Crown

Joann Stuebing, Grants Pass, Oregon

Ribbon Crown (four-patch pattern)

The delicate coloring in the quilt gives an old-fashioned feeling. It
is beautifully hand-quilted.

An Exhibit of Beautiful Traditional Quilts

Blackford's Beauty
Narrows Connection Quilt Guild, Gig Harbor,
Tacoma, and Fox Island, Washington
Blackford's Beauty (four-patch pattern)
Owner: Harriet Mooney, Fox Island, Washington
This is a very successful group scrap quilt.

Friends All Around

Ellen Anderson, Flagstaff, Arizona
Original Design
Movement, transparency, and depth have been created through
fabric and color placement. Blocks vary in size; filler blocks have
been added.

An Exhibit of Beautiful Traditional Quilts

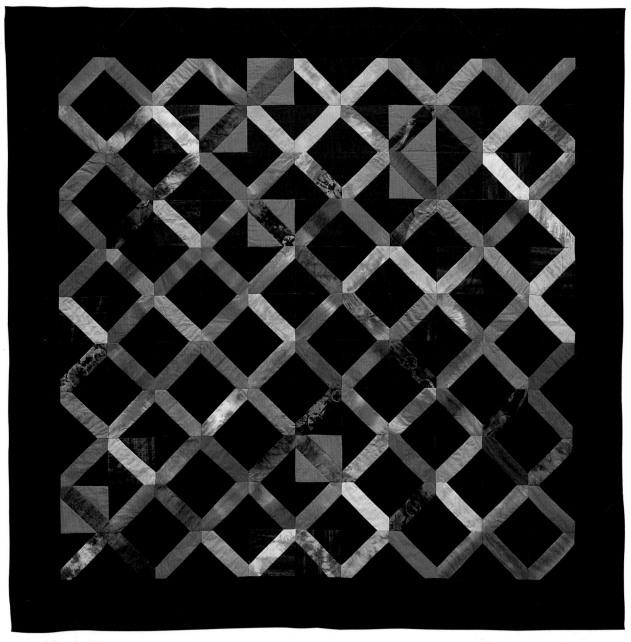

King's X

Sarah Dickson, San Antonio, Texas
King's X (four-patch pattern)
Hand dyed fabrics give this historic design a contemporary look.

Autumn Praise

Carol Webb, Tulsa, Oklahoma

Autumn Leaf Variation (five-patch pattern)

The fillers in the background provide more space than traditional settings; color and value choices enhance the quilt's beauty.

Bow Tie
Lynda Kelley, Tacoma, Washington
Bow Tie (four-patch pattern)
Colors and values create a three-dimensional effect.

Celebrating Fifty

Lynda Kelley, Tacoma, Washington

Churn Dash Variation (nine-patch pattern)

Strong color and texture use creates a very contemporary feeling.
Lynda made this quilt to celebrate her noteworthy birthday—using
fifty Churn Dash blocks to make her celebratory statement.

An Exhibit of Beautiful Traditional Quilts

Bow Tie

Lynda Kelley, Tacoma, Washington
Bow Tie (four-patch pattern)
This quilt has a very contemporary feeling with
Lynda's unique color and fabric choices.

Flock

Jodene Cook, Lebanon, Oregon
Flock (four-patch pattern)
The quilt's blocks have been placed in a barn-raising setting for
added interest.

An Exhibit of Beautiful Traditional Quilts

Tennessee Waltz

Diane Ebner, Phoenix, Arizona
Fifty-four-Forty or Fight/Snowball (nine-patch pattern)
Tennessee Waltz was inspired by a quilt seen in *Scrap Quilts*
by Judy Martin.

Alaskan Summer Nights

JoAnn Biegel, Anchorage, Alaska
Northwind (nine-patch pattern)
This quilt was inspired by the light skies during an Alaskan summer.
This design was inspired by the quilt *Pacific Nights* by Diana Voyer,
Victoria, British Columbia, Canada (QNM, December, 1991).

An Exhibit of Beautiful Traditional Quilts

Call me Moby.

Mary L. Gillis, Boston, Massachusetts
Storm at Sea variation (four-patch pattern)
Mary eliminated all repetitious side sections of the Storm at
Sea pattern. Inspired by a quilt created by Susan Varanka of
Meriden, Connecticut, whose quilt was shown on the back
cover of *Quilter's Newsletter Magazine*.

Chapter Four

Fantastic Five-Patch Patterns

Welcome to the five-patch pattern family! This is another fascinating group of block patterns. If you have been quilting for any length of time, you will be familiar with a few members of this small, but beloved family. Many wonderful five-patch patterns are unknown in our quilting world, as they are rarely published. Selected well-known and unusual patterns are included in this chapter's pattern collection. Also, some of my original five-patch patterns are presented here. Unlike the nine-patch and four-patch pattern families, the five-patch family has only two major divisions: the simple and complex five-patch pattern groups. I hope you will be inspired to use several of these interesting designs in your future projects.

Simple Five-Patch Patterns

(25-Square Grid Patterns)

As the name indicates, *simple five-patch patterns* are created from a grid using a division of five equal rows, horizontally and vertically. This grid uses twenty-five squares to form its designs (5 x 5 = 25).

25-Square Grid

Historic five-patch patterns using the simple twenty-five-square grid include Jack in the Box, Sister's Choice, Butterfly at the Crossroad, Flying Geese, Wedding Ring, Duck and Ducklings, Churn Dash, and Farmer's Daughter. Some of these can be seen in quilt settings on pages 82-84.

All patterns included in this group are very easy to draft, and they are equally easy to construct. They are excellent patterns to use if you are a novice quiltmaker.

Special Five-Patch Design Features

Some of the five-patch patterns are easily identified by their center bars, which are joined by a center square. The remaining design revolves around this central division. Simple five-patch blocks that use this design feature include Jack in the Box and Duck and Ducklings. A definite lattice pattern runs throughout each design when these blocks are set in multi-block designs; some may be seen on pages 82-84.

Sometimes this lattice effect is not noticeable when you look at only one pattern block (Flying Geese and Wedding Ring). However, when multiple blocks are set together, this design feature surprisingly appears. Notice how this happens in the traditional quilt settings of these blocks on pages 82 and 84.

Other five-patch designs do not have this strong feature. Instead, the gridding system allows for other design features to appear. This can result in very beautiful or dynamic quilts. When these blocks are placed in their settings, the overall designs visually excite us with the varied results, as shown on pages 83-85.

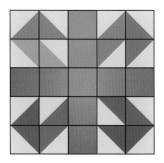 

Jack in the Box (Ruby McKim)

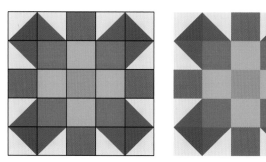

Sister's Choice (Ladies' Art Company #257, 1895)

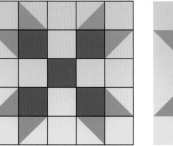 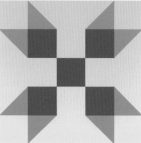

Butterfly at the Crossroad (Clara Stone)

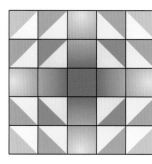 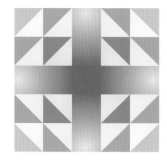

Flying Geese

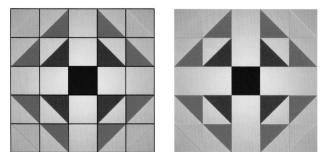

Wedding Ring (Ladies' Art Company #48, 1895)

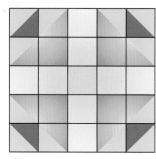 

Duck and Ducklings (Ladies' Art Company, 1898)

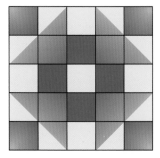 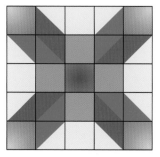

Churn Dash (Carrie Hall)

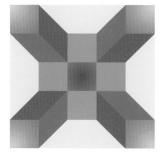

Farmer's Daughter (Clara Stone)

Drawing A Simple Five-Patch Pattern (25-Square Grid)

Before you draw your pattern, determine the block size. Next draw a square the exact size you wish your block to be (pages 15-16). For this exercise, we will use a 9" block. It needs a grid with five equal divisions, vertically and horizontally.

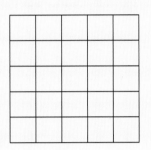

25-Square Grid

We begin by asking ourselves the following simple questions:

1. What size is my block? . . . . 9"

2. How many equal divisions do I need? 5

3. What number is larger than my block size and can be divided evenly by 5*? 10

   *Note: When determining this, always use the smallest possible number.

4. How many times does 5 go into 10? 2

After you have answered the above questions, proceed with the marking and drawing of the grid lines. To create these simple five-patch patterns, you will divide your drawn block into twenty-five equal squares by using the following instructions.

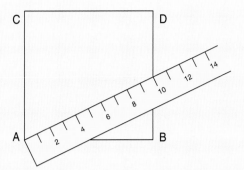

1. With your drawn 9" block in front of you, place the ruler's 0 mark exactly at corner A. Next, place the 10" mark of your ruler on the square's right vertical line B/D (10 is the answer to question #3 at left). (If your ruler marking will not fit on line B/D you will need to draw extension lines. See pages 78-81 for detailed instructions.)

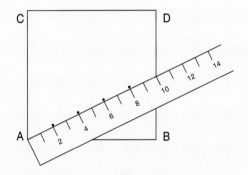

2. Make a mark every 2" along the ruler edge (2 is the answer to question #4 at left). In this example, you will make a mark at the 2", 4", 6", and 8" ruler markings.

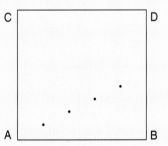

3. Your marks divide the block into five equal divisions.

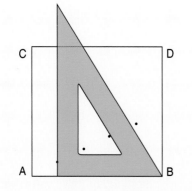

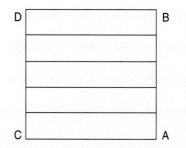

4. Place the drafting triangle on your block's baseline A/B, lining it up to the first pencil mark. Using the baseline and mark as reference points, draw the first grid line. Continue drawing grid lines, using the reference marks.

7. Rotate your paper one-quarter turn. Line C/A should now be at the bottom of the page, directly in front of you.

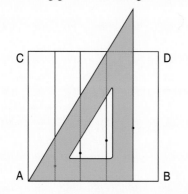

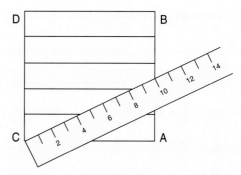

5. As you work on the right side of your block, flip the triangle over so the 90-degree angle is placed on the block's right side.

8. Now repeat the same procedure. Place the ruler's 0 mark at corner C. Place the 10" mark at the right-hand vertical line A/B.

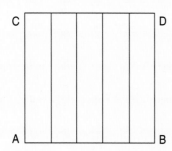

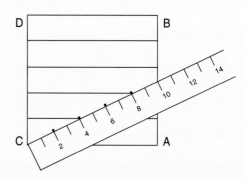

6. When you have drawn vertical lines for all the markings, you will have your first set of grid lines.

9. Mark every 2" along the ruler. Again, these markings will be at the 2", 4", 6", and 8" ruler markings.

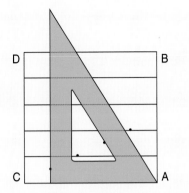

10. With the drafting triangle placed on line C/A, draw the vertical lines at each marking.

11. When you have drawn these lines, you will have a perfect twenty-five-square grid to draft your pattern.

With your pattern in front of you, draw its design lines, square by square. Use a colored pencil to draw the pattern so the grid and pattern lines do not get mixed up.

When you have drawn this custom-made graph paper, remember you can draw any simple five-patch pattern you choose. You may use this grid to draw any pattern included in this chapter or a pattern from any other publication.

Complex Five-Patch Patterns

(100-Square Grid Patterns)

As in other pattern families, you will need additional reference points and grid lines to create many five-patch designs. Many lovely five-patch patterns need ten horizontal and vertical divisions. The grid, then, is made from 100 squares (10 x 10 = 100). Patterns made from this grid are *complex five-patch patterns.*

100-Square Grid

Mexican Cross has been a favorite historic complex five-patch pattern for many decades. Wonderful lesser-known patterns include Dutch Mill, King David's Crown, Golden Royalty, Cross and Crown and Bachelor's Puzzle.

Many historic five-patch patterns create added interest when the blocks are put together. Illusions of depth, luster, luminosity, shadows, and highlights can be created in these blocks with fascinating results. Bachelor's Puzzle, Mexican Cross, and Dutch Mill have great illusionary potential. Notice their interesting overall designs on pages 82-84.

Because I like the five-patch complex grid so much, I have designed several patterns in this pattern family. I have included a few here. Around the Corner has a traditional flavor. Designs with the illusion of curves include Starry Roundabout, Imaginary Curves, and Poinsettia in Bloom (Chapter Six, page 104).

Patterns with strong layering possibilities include Glowing Stars and Gems and Beyond the Reef. Most of these new patterns can promote the illusions of depth, luster and luminosity. I hope you will play with a few of these patterns. Some of the complex five-patch patterns included in this chapter can be seen in their multiple-block settings on pages 82-85.

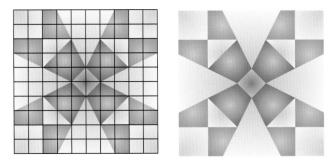

Dutch Mill (Ladies' Art Company #451, 1922)

King David's Crown (Carrie Hall, 1935)

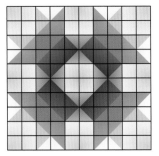

Golden Royalty

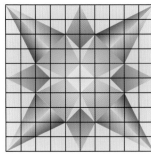

Sparkling Jewels (Joen Wolfrom, 1997)

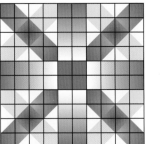

Bachelor's Puzzle (Ladies' Art Company, 1898)

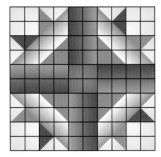

Cross and Crown

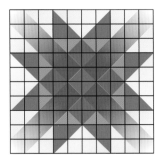

Mexican Cross

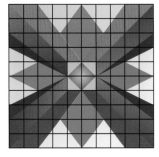

Beyond the Reef (Joen Wolfrom, 1995)

Make Any Block Any Size

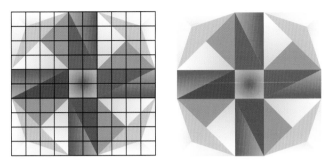

Around the Corner (Joen Wolfrom, 1997)

Glowing Stars and Gems (Joen Wolfrom, 1992)

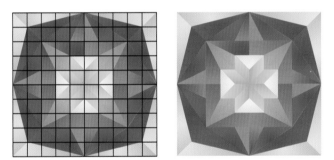

Starry Roundabout (Joen Wolfrom, 1997)

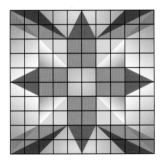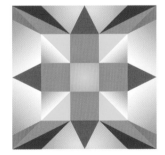

Imaginary Curves (Joen Wolfrom, 1997)

Drawing A Complex Five-Patch Pattern (100-Square Grid)

If you wish to use a complex five-patch pattern, you will need to customize your pattern's grid with ten equal divisions, horizontally and vertically (100-square grid).

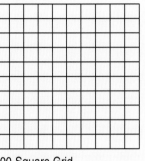

100-Square Grid

Determine your block size and the pattern you wish to use. Draw the square to its exact size (pages 15-16). To illustrate this group's drawing exercise, we will use a 12" block. To begin, we ask ourselves the following questions:

1. What size is my block? . . . . 12"

2. How many equal divisions do I need? 10

3. What number is larger than the block size and can be divided evenly by 10?* 20

    *Note: When determining this, always use the smallest possible number.

4. How many times does 10 go into 20? 2

After you have determined the answers to the above questions, you will proceed with drawing the block and marking the grid lines. To create these comples five-patch patterns, you will divide your drawn block into 100 divisions using the following instructions.

Often you can proceed in the same manner as shown in the simple five-patch pattern. Sometimes, however, you will need to add extension lines to your block's perimeter before proceeding. Therefore, this example will be done using extension lines so you will be familiar with this procedure when it is needed.

Adding Extension Lines

To make extensions for any patch pattern proceed with the following instructions.*

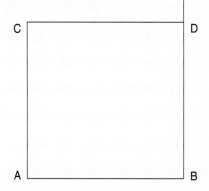

1. Sometimes it is impossible to place the ruler on the right-hand vertical line at the selected inch marking. This primarily happens when a block needs to be divided into many divisions or when the block is small. If you find it is impossible to place your ruler marking on the block's vertical perimeter line B/D, extend the line past the block's boundary. Extend it accurately with a drafting triangle, so it remains perpendicular to line A/B.

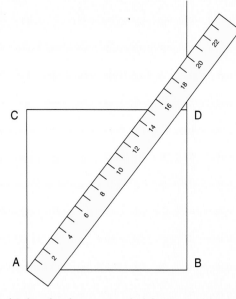

2. Once this line has been extended, begin positioning your ruler on the square. In our selected example (page 77), the block size is 12" and our complex five-patch pattern needs ten equal divisions. The number 20 is both larger than the block size and can be divided evenly by 10. Therefore, with the 12" square in front of you, place the ruler's 0 mark at corner A. Next place your ruler's 20" mark (answer to question #3 on page 77) on the square's extended right vertical line B/D.

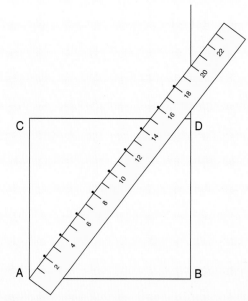

3. Mark every 2" along the ruler edge (20 divided by 10 = 2, the answer to question #4 on page 17). In this example, you will make a mark at the 2", 4", 6", 8", 10", 12", 14", 16", and 18" ruler markings. Notice the 16" and 18" markings are outside the square's perimeter line. Do not be alarmed when this happens. They are the reference points for those grid lines.

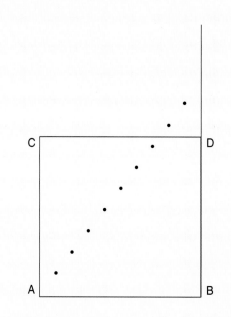

4. This will divide the block into ten equal divisions.

* Note: If you have been referred to this section from another chapter, use the specific numbers that apply to your selected pattern and its grid, rather than the ones used in this example, unless you wish to practice with the complex five-patch pattern example.

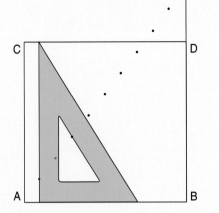

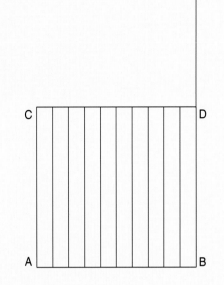

5. Place the drafting triangle on your block's baseline A/B, lining it up to the first pencil mark. Draw the first grid line. Continue drawing each of these vertical grid lines, lining the drafting triangle up with each grid-line mark.

7. You have now completed your first set of grid lines.

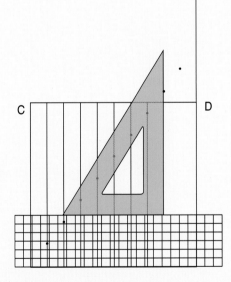

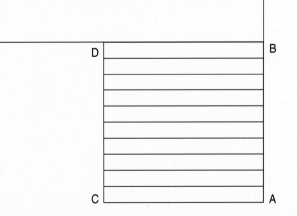

6. To reach the marks made above the block you may have to move the drafting triangle. Make certain the triangle stays parallel to the baseline A/B when changing the triangle's position. Place a wide ruler on line A/B and then place the triangle against the ruler so you can adjust the triangle's position.

8. Rotate the paper one-quarter turn, so the baseline is now line C/A. Draw an extension line on the right-hand vertical line A/B.

Fantastic Five-Patch Patterns

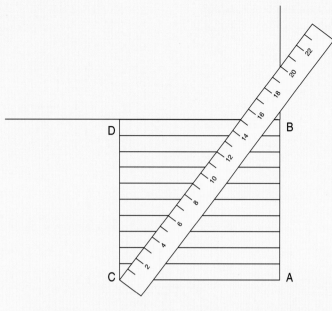

9. Next place the 0 mark of the ruler on corner C and then place the ruler's 20" mark on extended line A/B.

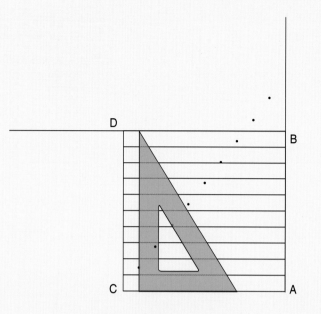

11. With the drafting triangle placed on line C/A and using the marks as reference points, begin drawing the vertical lines at each marking on the left side.

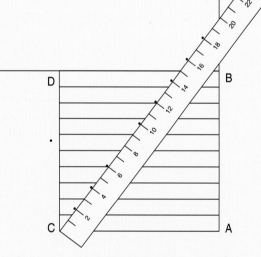

10. Mark the reference points as you did in the first set of grid lines. You will mark at the 2", 4", 6", 8", 10", 12", 14", 16", and 18" marks. Again, the last two marks will lie outside the drawn square. These are the reference points for the last four grid lines.

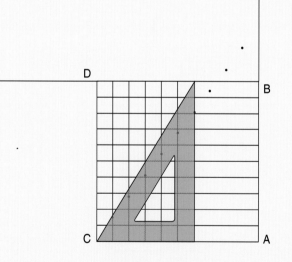

12. When you are drawing the right-hand side grid lines, flip the drafting triangle, so its 90-degree side is on the square's right-hand side.

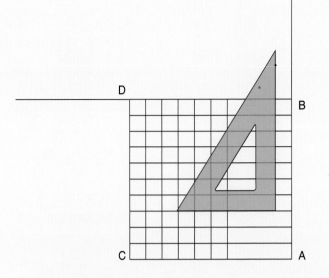

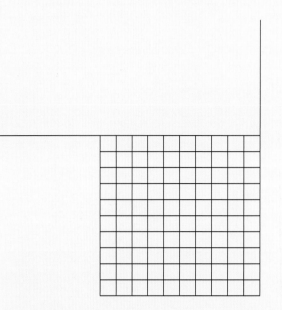

13. To reach the marks made above the block, move the drafting triangle to a previously drawn horizontal grid line, using it as an adjusted baseline. Draw the top portions of these lines with the drafting triangle lined up with the outer markings and the adjusted baseline.

15. When you have completed drawing your grid lines, you will have a perfect 100-square grid.

With your pattern in front of you, draw its design lines in this custom gridded square. Use a colored pencil to draw the pattern lines, so the grid and pattern lines do not get mixed up. You may select any complex five-patch pattern to draft with this customized grid.

Multiple Block Quilt Settings

It is very important to know how your pattern evolves when multiple blocks are placed together in a quilt. It is almost always impossible to predict the overall pattern simply by looking at only one block. Therefore, I have included traditional settings for many of the five-patch patterns in this chapter on pages 82-85.

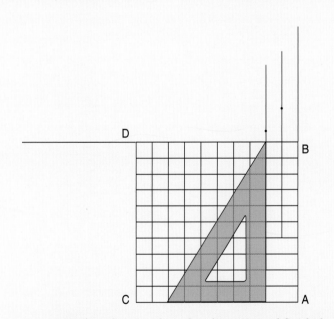

14. Next place the triangle on baseline C/A and finish drawing the bottom portions of the grid lines. Be sure to match the top and bottom grid lines perfectly.

Duck and Ducklings

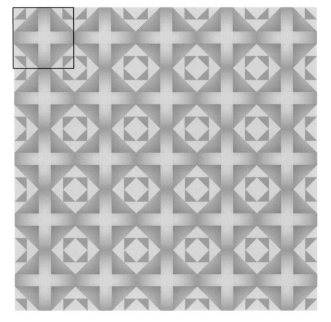

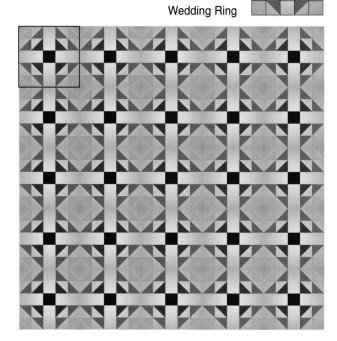

Wedding Ring

Churn Dash: Setting Variation

Bachelor's Puzzle

Five-Patch

Farmer's Daughter

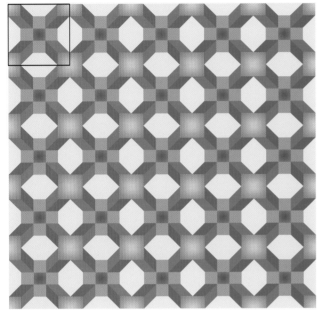

Jack in the Box

Mexican Cross

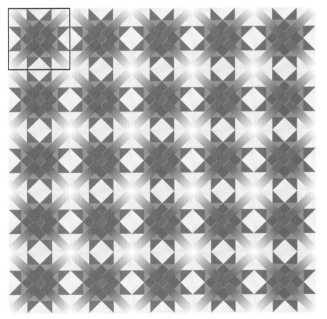

Beyond the Reef

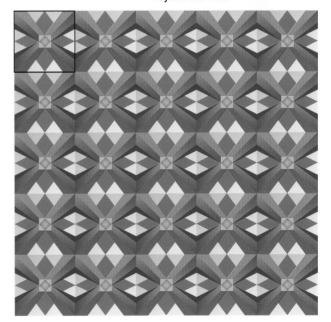

Dutch Mill

Sparkling Jewels

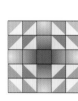

Flying Geese

Butterfly at the Crossroad

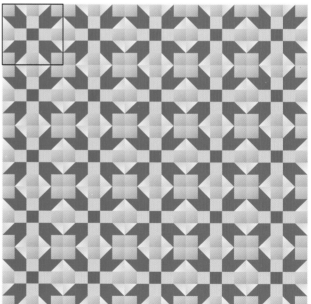

Cross and Crown

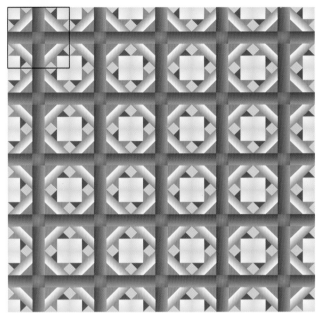

Around the Corner

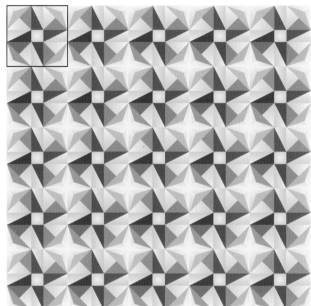

Starry Roundabout

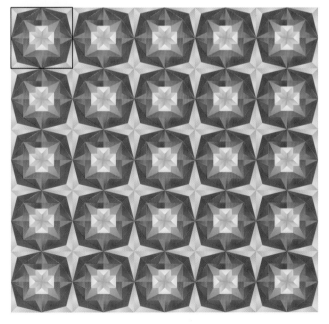

Glowing Stars and Gems

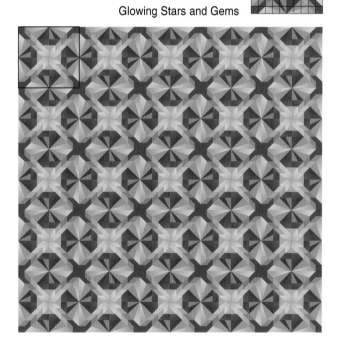

Fantastic Five-Patch Patterns

Chapter Five
Spectacular Seven-Patch Patterns

I really enjoy working with the seven-patch pattern family. This small little-known family is rarely used in quilts. Regardless of this, the seven-patch pattern family includes some of the most beautiful pattern options. Fantastic designs can evolve with their custom grid. The seven-patch pattern family is divided into two groups: simple and complex seven-patch patterns.

Simple Seven-Patch Patterns

(49-Square Grid Patterns)

Simple seven-patch patterns use a grid of seven equal divisions horizontally and vertically. This gives a grid of forty-nine squares in which you will create these designs (7 x 7 = 49).

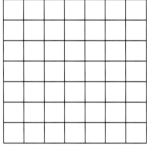

49-Square Grid

Although seven-patch patterns are not numerous, a few have been long-time traditional favorites. These include Bear's Paw, Hen and Chickens, Dove in the Window, and Chain of Friendship. Another historic seven-patch pattern is Stone Mason's Puzzle, which creates interesting depth.

Probably the most frequently-made historic seven-patch pattern is Bear's Paw. Two different renditions are created by Joann Stuebing and JoAnn Biegel (photo pages 12 and 57). Because I enjoy the seven-patch family so much, I have designed numerous patterns using this forty-nine-square grid.

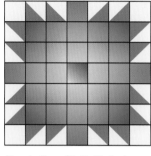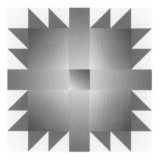

Bear's Paw (Ruth Finley)

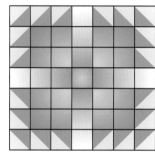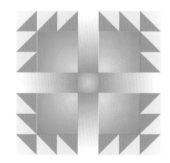

Hen and Chickens (Ladies' Art Company)

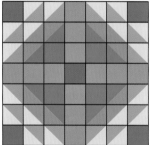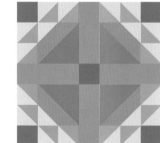

Dove in the Window (Ladies' Art Company #215, 1895)

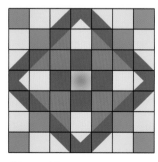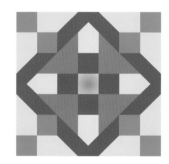

Chain of Friendship

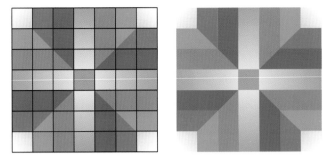

Stone Mason's Puzzle (Ladies' Art Company #457, 1922)

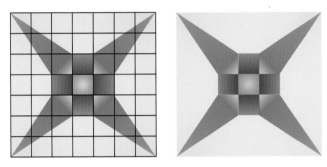

Star Light-Star Bright (Joen Wolfrom, 1997)

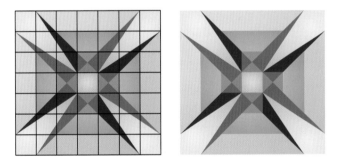

Star Stretch (Joen Wolfrom, 1997)

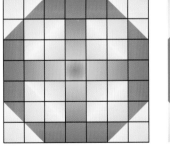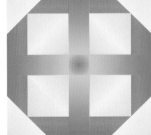

Windows of Light (Joen Wolfrom, 1997)

Drawing A Simple Seven-Patch Pattern (49-Square Grid)

After you select the seven-patch pattern you wish to use, determine its block size. Draw your block to this exact size (pages 15-16). Look closely at the block design you have chosen. This simple seven-patch block will need seven equal divisions both horizontally and vertically.

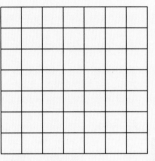

49-Square Grid

For learning purposes, we will use a 12" block. We need to divide the twelve-inch square into seven equal parts, horizontally and vertically. We begin by asking ourselves the following simple questions:

1. What size is my block? . . . . 12"

2. How many equal divisions are needed? 7

3. What number can be divided by 7 and
   is larger than the block size?* 14

   *Note: When determining this, always use the smallest possible number.

4. How many times does 7 go into 14? 2

After you have determined the answers to the above questions, proceed with the marking and the drawing of the grid lines. To create these simple seven-patch patterns, you will divide your drawn block into forty-nine equal squares, using the following instructions.

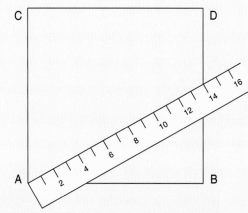

1. With the drawn 12" square in front of you, begin marking your block's first set of seven equal divisions. Place the ruler's 0 mark at corner A. Next, place the 14" mark of your ruler on the square's right vertical line B/D (14 is the answer to question #3 listed on page 87). (If your ruler marking will not fit on line B/D, you will need to draw extension lines. See pages 78-81 for detailed instructions.)

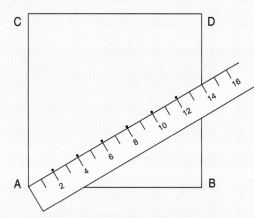

2. Mark every 2" along the ruler edge (14 divided by 7 = 2, the answer to #4 on page 87). In this example, you will make a mark at the 2", 4", 6", 8", 10", and 12" ruler markings.

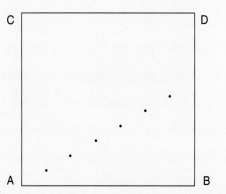

3. Your markings will divide the square into seven equal divisions.

4. Place the drafting triangle on line A/B, lining it up with the first dot. Using the baseline and dot as reference points, draw the first grid line. Next, draw the second grid line at the 4" ruler marking. Continue drawing these grid lines.

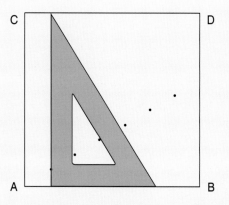

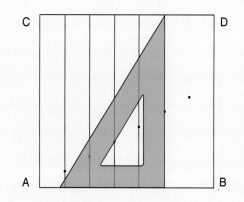

5. As you work on the right side of your block, flip the triangle over, so the 90-degree angle is on the square's right side.

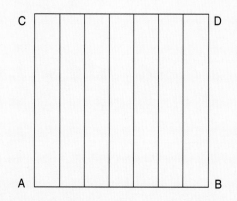

6. After the last line has been drawn, the first set of grid lines has been made.

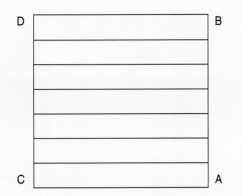

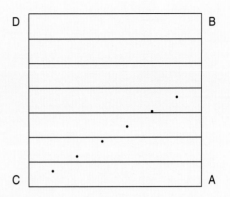

7. Rotate your paper one-quarter turn. Line C/A should now be at the bottom of the page, directly in front of you.

10. You can see these markings divide your square into seven equal parts.

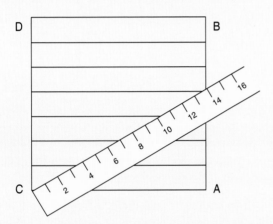

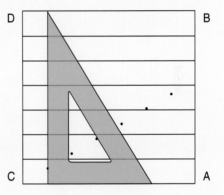

8. Repeat the process. Place the ruler's 0 mark at corner C. Place the 14" mark at the right-hand vertical line A/B.

11. With the drafting triangle placed on line C/A and using the dots as reference points, draw vertical lines at each marking, beginning at the 2" mark.

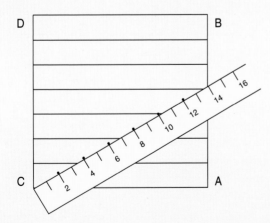

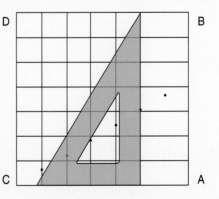

9. Mark every 2" along the ruler. Again, you will have made pencil marks at the 2", 4", 6", 8", 10", and 12" markings.

12. When drawing the right-hand grid lines, flip the drafting triangle over, so its 90-degree angle is on the square's right side.

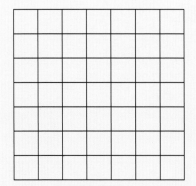

13. When you have completed drawing these lines, you will have a perfect 49-square grid from which to draft your pattern.

With your pattern in front of you, draw its design lines, square by square. Use a sharp colored pencil to draw the pattern, so the grid and pattern lines do not get mixed up. When you have finished drawing your lines, your pattern will appear.

Complex Seven-Patch Patterns
(196-Square Grid Patterns)

Many beautiful seven-patch patterns need more than the simple grid to create their designs. They need a grid of fourteen equal divisions, horizontally and vertically. This results in a grid of 196 squares (14 x 14 = 196). These designs are *complex seven-patch patterns.*

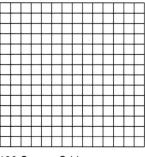

196-Square Grid

Although this sounds like a lot of squares, it is simply a grid to provide the needed reference points to create your pattern. This grid gives us a wonderful format for designing interesting patterns.

In this chapter, I have included eight of my own complex seven-patch patterns. Star Trek, Peacock Dance, Through the Looking Glass, Diamond Weave, Star Flash, and Hidden Star have strong diagonal designs and allow dimensional play. Australian Gemstone was inspired by my visit to that awesome continent. Star Burst is one of my favorite designs, because it creates such an interesting three-dimensional effect.

Seven-Patch

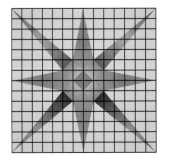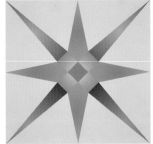

Star Trek (Joen Wolfrom, 1997)

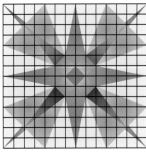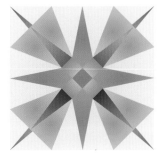

Peacock Dance (Joen Wolfrom, 1997)

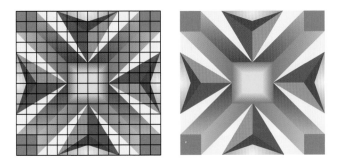

Through the Looking Glass (Joen Wolfrom, 1994)

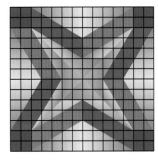

Diamond Weave (Joen Wolfrom, 1997)

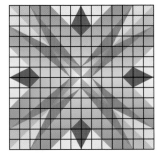

Star Flash (Joen Wolfrom, 1997)

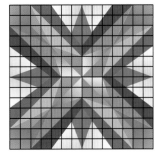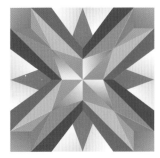

Hidden Star (Joen Wolfrom, 1996)

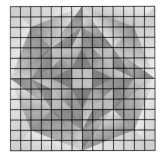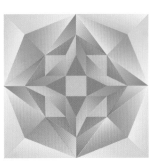

Australian Gemstone (Joen Wolfrom, 1997)

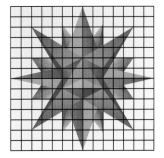

Starburst (Joen Wolfrom, 1997)

Spectacular Seven-Patch Patterns

Drawing A Complex Seven-Patch Pattern (196-Square Grid)

If you would like to create a quilt using any of the complex seven-patch patterns, use the following instructions. First, determine your block size and the pattern you wish to use. Draw the square to its exact size (pages 15-16). All complex seven-patch patterns need a grid made from fourteen equal divisions, horizontally and vertically.

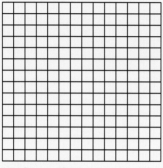

196-Square Grid

For learning purposes we will use an 11" block. To begin, we ask ourselves the following questions:

1. What size is my block? . . . . 11"

2. How many equal divisions do I need? 14

3. What number is larger than my block size, and can be divided by 14?* 14

   *Note: When determining this, always use the smallest possible number.

4. How many times does 14 go into 14? 1

After you have determined the answers to the above questions, proceed with the marking and drawing of the grid lines. To create these complex seven-patch patterns, you will divide your drawn block into 196 equal squares, using the following instructions.

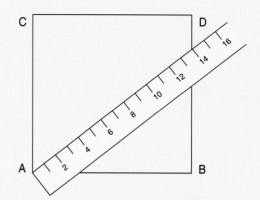

1. With an 11" square in front of you, place the ruler's 0 mark exactly at corner A. Next, place the 14" (answer to #3) mark of your ruler on the square's right vertical line B/D. (If your ruler marking will not fit on line B/D you will need to draw extension lines. See pages 78-81 for detailed instructions.)

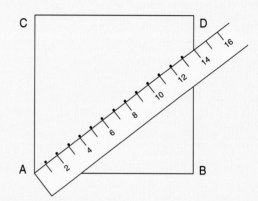

2. Mark every 1" along the ruler edge (14 divided by 14 = 1, the answer to #4).

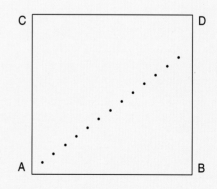

3. These marks will divide the square into fourteen equal divisions.

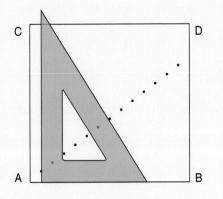

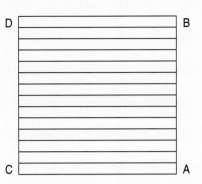

4. Place the drafting triangle on your block's baseline A/B, lining it up to the first mark. Draw the first grid line. Next, draw the next grid line at the second ruler marking.

7. Rotate your paper one-quarter turn. Line C/A should be at the bottom of the page, directly in front of you.

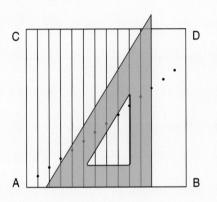

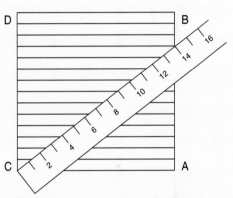

5. As you work along the right side of your block, flip the triangle over, so the 90-degree angle is on the square's right side. Continue until you have drawn lines for all of your markings.

8. Repeat the previous process. Place the ruler's 0 mark at corner C. Place the 14" mark at the right-hand vertical line A/B.

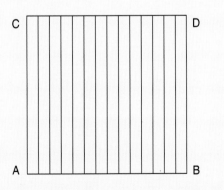

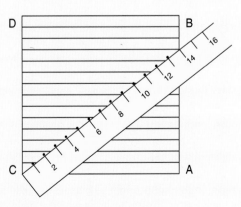

6. You have now completed the first set of grid lines.

9. Again, mark every 1" along the ruler.

Spectacular Seven-Patch Patterns

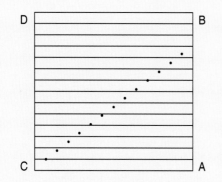

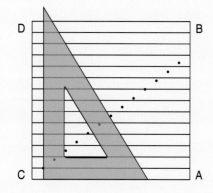

10. With these marks, the square has been divided into fourteen equal divisions.

11. With the drafting triangle placed on line C/A and using the dots as reference points, draw vertical lines at each marking.

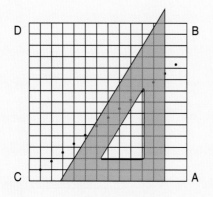

12. When drawing the right-side grid lines, flip the drafting triangle over, so its 90-degree angle is on the square's right side.

13. When you have drawn these lines, you will have a perfect 196-square grid customized for any complex seven-patch pattern.

With your pattern in front of you, draw its design lines in your gridded block's square. Use a colored pencil to draw the pattern so the grid and pattern lines do not get mixed up. When you have finished drawing these lines, you will have a perfect line drawing of your block.

Multiple Block Quilt Settings

You can view some of this chapter's patterns in their overall designs on pages 95-97. (Climbing Nasturtium, another complex seven-patch pattern, can be seen in Chapter Six, page 102.) Some of these patterns can be challenging, but their beautiful overall designs will make them worth the extra effort.

Bear's Paw

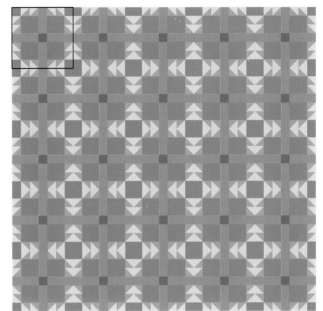

Dove in the Window

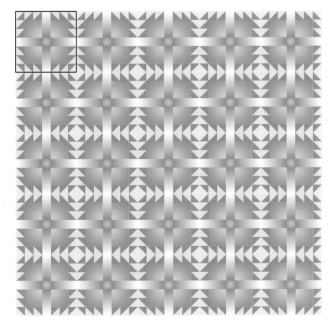

Hen and Chickens

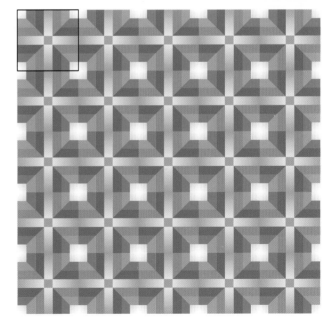

Stone Mason's Puzzle

Seven-Patch

Star Light-Star Bright

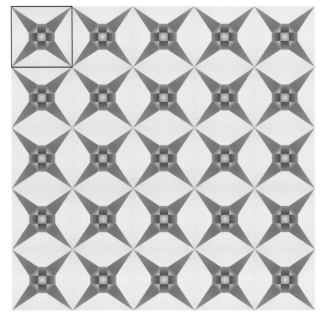

Star Trek

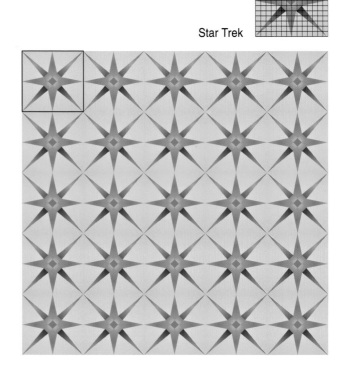

 Star Stretch

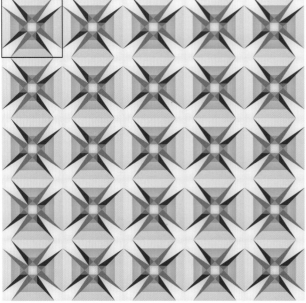

Peacock Dance

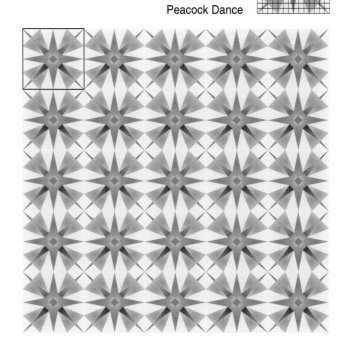

Make Any Block Any Size

96

Through the Looking Glass

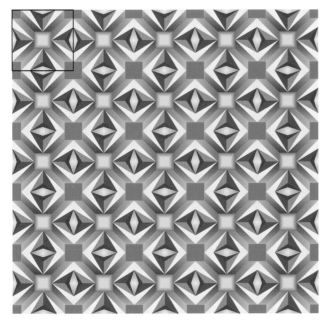

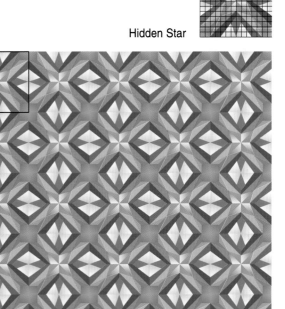

Hidden Star

Diamond Weave

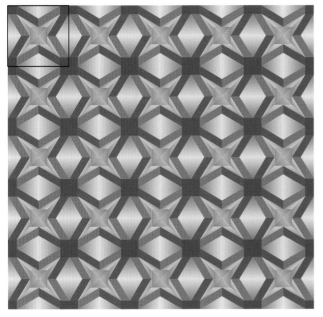

Starburst

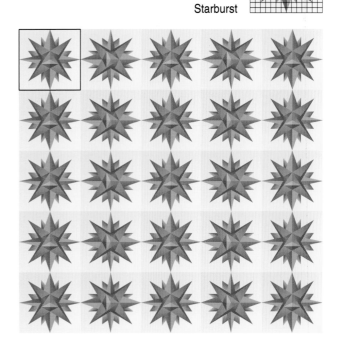

Spectacular Seven-Patch Patterns

Chapter Six
Enticing Patterns for Special Quilts

The patterns in this chapter are unique, because each works within a special theme. While some of these patterns fit into one of the previously mentioned patch-pattern families, some are created with their own unique gridding system.

Sailing

The pattern Sailboat, a historic traditional pattern, can be designed from a simple four-patch pattern.

I made a quilt from this pattern for my elder son years ago. After making it, I felt the pattern could be enhanced by slightly redesigning it. In doing so, I have chosen to place it in the five-patch family's simple grid.

The new pattern, Sailing Away, has a bit more height than the historic pattern.

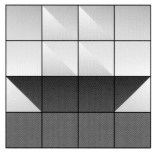

Sailboat

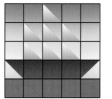 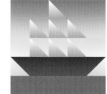

Sailing Away

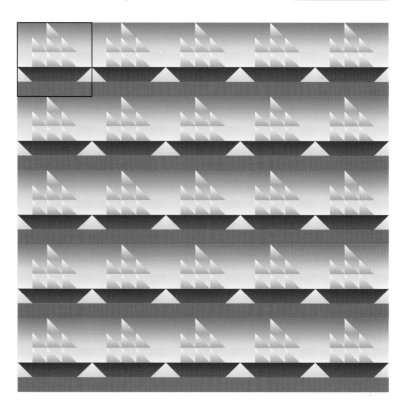

Houses

House quilts are very popular today. There are several historic house patterns available. You can have lots of fun creating your own too. I have made my own house pattern, although it does not resemble any house I have lived in. I call this pattern Back Home.

My gridding system is a bit unusual. I have divided each block into nine horizontal divisions and twenty-four vertical divisions. This uneven grid allows more flexibility with the pattern.

Incidentally, you will notice one horizontal grid is divided into two sections. I did this so I could place the horizon line (where the land and sky meet) exactly where I wanted it. I didn't want to set the horizon line along the same grid line as any house lines. Thus I purposely drew the separation between land and sky between two grid lines. You could choose to place the horizon line lower, higher, or on a horizontal grid line, if you wish.

The houses are placed in a square block, a vertical rectangle, and a horizontal rectangle. This results in tall houses, elongated houses, and stocky houses. The blocks' widths differ while their heights are the same. Working with block variations creates more interest in the overall design than if all blocks were identical. Using different fabrics for each house creates even more variations in the overall design.

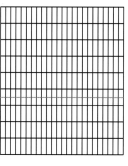

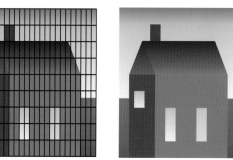

Placed in a vertical rectangle.

Placed in a square block

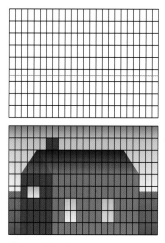

Placed in a horizontal rectangle.

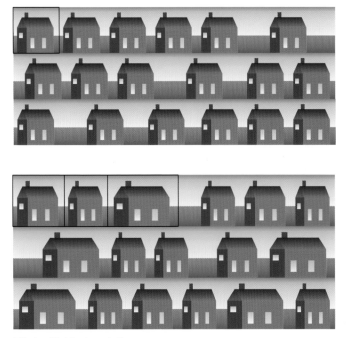

Work with block variations.

Fillers

Notice I have used fillers to break up the spaces between some of the house blocks. Fillers can be any width. They are used to fill up any spaces needed within a row. They provide greater flexibility in placing your houses in rows, as they can be used to fill up uneven spaces. They also allow for visual relief. In addition, you can use these fillers as places to add plants, flowers, and other nature details. This creates more interest.

To construct, work in straight lines. There will be times when it makes sense to construct pieces together vertically. At other times, you may want to sew pieces together in a horizontal section. Putting the pattern together is like working on a puzzle.

If you build your own house, create a grid that best suits the scene you would like to design. Ellen Anderson has created a most wonderful house quilt, *Friends All Around* (page 61), in which she has made a wide variety of houses. Also, she has changed the blocks' sizes and added fillers. A barn creates even more contrast and visual relief.

Flowers

I love flowers and gardening. Therefore, I am interested in designing many different flower patterns. Two of my favorite historic flower patterns are Rosebud, a seven-patch pattern, and Nosegay, a four-patch pattern. Many of my own older flower patterns are reminiscent of historic patterns. Spring Anemone is a complex five-patch pattern with ten equal divisions, horizontally and vertically. Blooming Poppy II is another complex five-patch pattern. Climbing Nasturtium (page 102) is a complex seven-patch pattern with fourteen equal divisions horizontally and vertically. Tulip Blossoms (page 102) is a pattern using a grid of twenty-one equal divisions, horizontally and vertically.

Trumpeter's Glory (page 102) is a modernistic pattern, paying tribute to the wonderful flowers that courageously break the grayness of winter as they burst into the hope of spring. This pattern is designed in a vertical rectangle. There are twenty-five equal vertical divisions and thirty-four equal horizontal divisions. Once this grid has been made, you can easily draw the pattern by following the flowers' pattern lines. The background can be broken into any shapes you wish. I have chosen to divide the background into the shapes shown, but many other divisions are possible. The more the background is broken up, the greater interest will be achieved.

This pattern would make an excellent center for a medallion-style quilt. If each grid square equaled one-inch, the medallion center would be 25" wide by 34" high.

Always try to piece in straight lines. Also, work in sections or units. Then put these larger units together. There are innumerable ways you can piece this pattern together. Begin where you feel most comfortable. Work in the manner that seems most sensible to you.

Spring Anemone
(Joen Wolfrom, 1994)

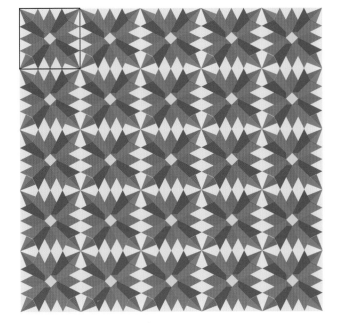

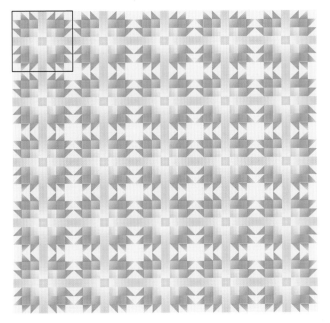

Rosebud
(Aunt Martha)

Blooming Poppy II
(Joen Wolfrom, 1998)

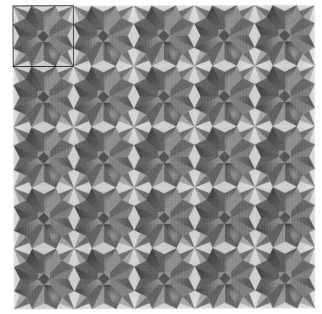

Nosegay
(variation of Nosegay Quilt
from Rural New Yorker, 1933)

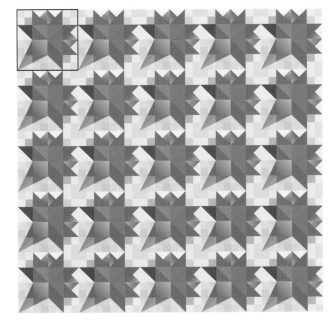

Special Blocks

Enticing Patterns for Special Quilts

Climbing Nasturtium
(Joen Wolfrom, 1997)

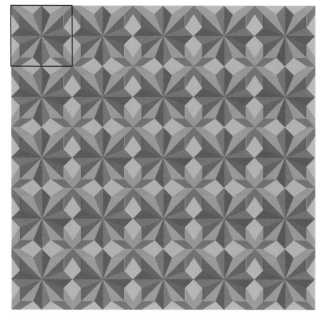

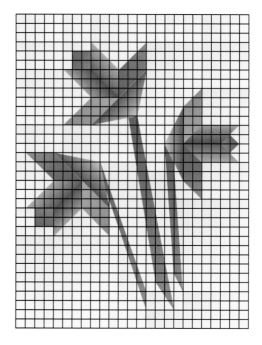

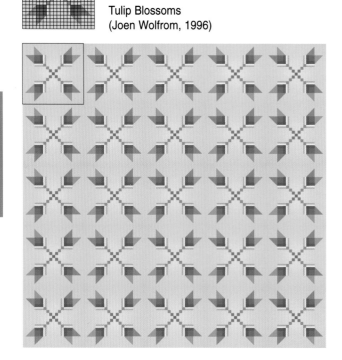

Tulip Blossoms
(Joen Wolfrom, 1996)

Trumpeter's Glory
(Joen Wolfrom, 1997)

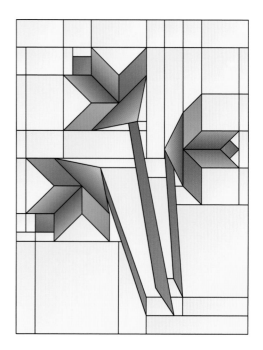

Special Blocks

Leaves

Leaf quilts are quite popular. There are several historic leaf patterns available. One of the easiest to construct is Maple Leaf, a simple nine-patch pattern.

Instead of putting the blocks in the traditional setting, as shown here, think about making some simple changes. Add fillers to the background to give your leaves a greater feeling of freedom. This also allows you to play with the background. Rotate the blocks, so the leaves appear to be falling to the ground. Change the colors and values of the leaves, so each leaf is unique. This will create wonderful visual interest. Use dozens of fabrics to reproduce the subtle variations of colors, textures, and values of autumn.

Autumn Days is a contemporary leaf block I have created. It is shown with the blocks rotated. For your own quilt, you may want to rotate the blocks, change the fabrics and values in each block, and add background fillers. In addition, consider enhancing your design by staggering the blocks. This creates more design flexibility. For detailed instructions on staggering blocks, see *Patchwork Persuasion*, pages 95 and 96 (by the author).

Two exquisite leaf quilts are Autumn Praise (page 63) by Carol Webb and Fall's Folly (page 8) by Debbie Wertmann. Each is unique in its presentation and coloration.

Maple Leaf
(Clara Stone)

Autumn Days
(Joen Wolfrom, 1997)

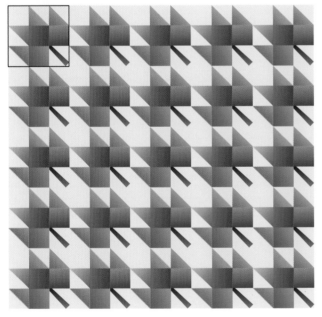

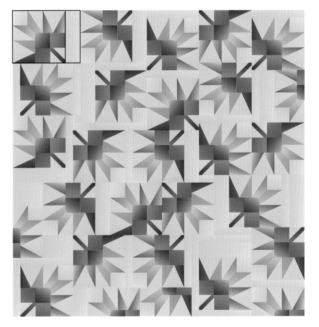

Special Blocks

Winter Holidays

Winter holidays are important to most of us. I have included three patterns of my own design as a special tribute to this time of year. The first, Poinsettia in Bloom, is a complex five-patch pattern with ten equal divisions, horizontally and vertically. When the pattern is set in multiple blocks a circular pattern evolves.

Star Wreath uses a grid of eighteen equal divisions, horizontally and vertically. This star, wrapped in a wreath, can be colored to evoke a sense of shadows and highlights. When the pattern is put into a multiple-block design a small secondary star is created. Although I have not colored this in traditional holiday colors, it would be beautiful in deep forest greens, a touch of soft gold, and rich reds, plums, and maroons.

Poinsettia in Bloom
(Joen Wolfrom, 1997)

Star Wreath
(Joen Wolfrom, 1997)

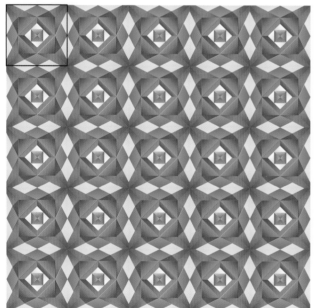

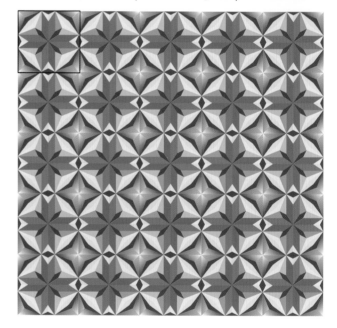

Candles of Joy uses a combination of piecing and appliqué techniques. The grid used is an intricate four-patch grid; sixteen equal divisions, horizontally and vertically. Add diagonal lines to your block to help you place the candles in their center position. Once you have drawn these lines and the grid lines, begin drawing the outer block design. Piece the block in your favorite manner.

After the block has been constructed, draw your candles. I have designed six candles for the cluster. Feel free to change the number of candles. Each candle should vary in shape, color, size, and texture. Even the candle flames can be varied slightly in shape, size, and color.

Once you have decided on their placement, hand or machine appliqué them to the block. You can use this design in a multiple-block quilt or as a medallion center.

Conclusion

Enjoy creating any of these blocks—or have fun designing your own blocks, using any grid system that works for you. All of these blocks can be easily drawn. First determine the block size. Draw the square. Then determine how many divisions are needed, horizontally and vertically. Use the drawing method described in the earlier chapters to create your grid lines. After the grid lines have been created, begin drawing your design. When your design lines are all drawn, you will have a perfect pattern from which to work.

Candles of Joy

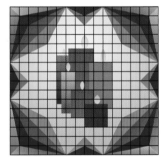

Candles of Joy (Joen Wolfrom, 1997)

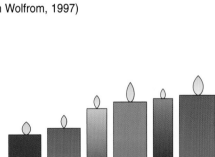

Candles and Flames

Chapter Seven

Exciting Quilts Using Block Blends

Blending Blocks from Patch Families

Often two blocks from the same pattern family can be combined to create a beautiful, new overall design. This unique marriage of blocks is called *blending blocks* or *block blends*. Successful blending occurs when blocks are well united to each other. Basic, simple, and complex patterns from the same family can blend very well with each other. Many patterns are enhanced beautifully by combining with another block. In a blended partnership you will find wonderful, exciting new patterns evolving.

In this chapter I have blended scores of blocks for your use. There are samplings from all the patch-families represented here. It is exciting to see how well the patterns work together. The design opportunities seem endless. Have fun working with these block blends.

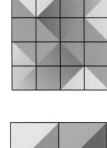

Whirlwind and
Making Waves

Blends

Amazing Four-Patch Pattern Blends

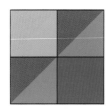

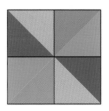

Birds in the Air
and Pinwheel

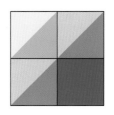

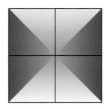

Birds in the Air
and Yankee Puzzle

Exciting Quilts Using Block Blends

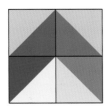

Streak of Lightning
and Birds in the Air

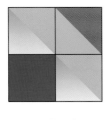

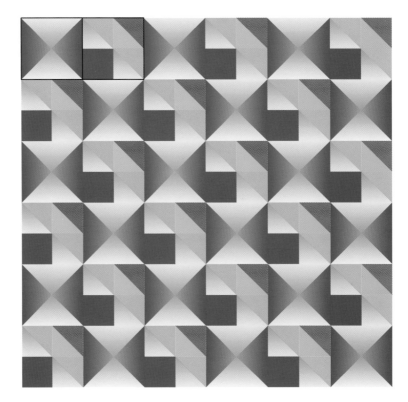

Yankee Puzzle
and Birds in the Air

Make Any Block Any Size

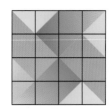

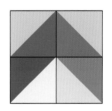

Whirlwind and
Streak of Lightning

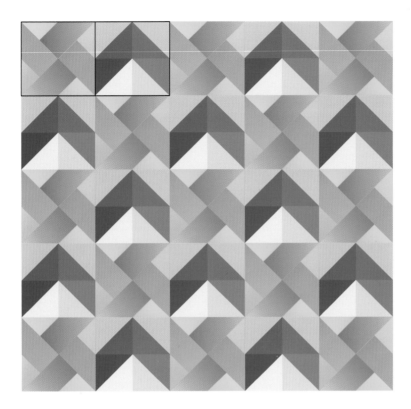

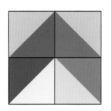

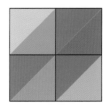

Streak of Lightning
and Making Waves

Exciting Quilts Using Block Blends

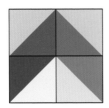

Streak of Lightning
and Yankee Puzzle

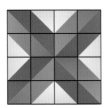

King's X and
Celebration

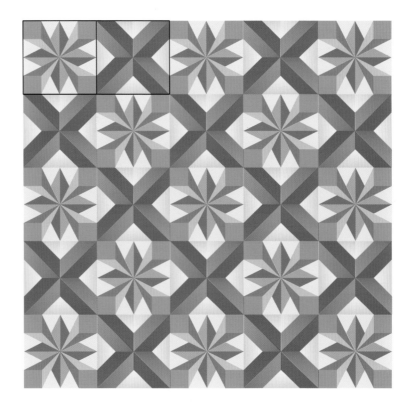

Make Any Block Any Size

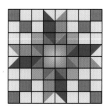

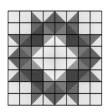

Stepping Stones and
Laurel Wreath

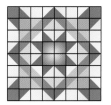

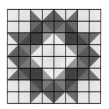

Nancy's Fancy and
Laurel Wreath

Exciting Quilts Using Block Blends

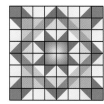

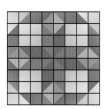

Nancy's Fancy and
Rolling Star

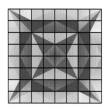

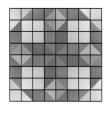

Echoes
and Rolling Star

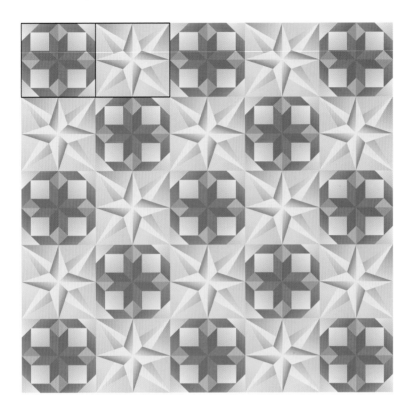

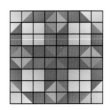

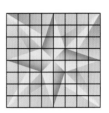

Rolling Star and
Fleeting Star

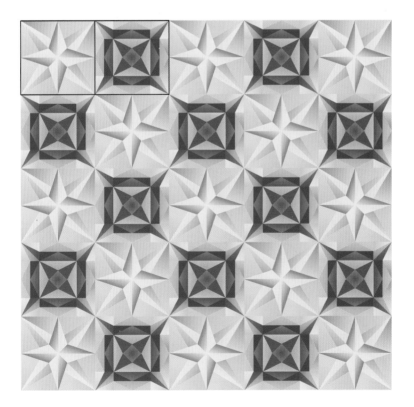

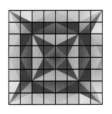

Fleeting Star
and Echoes

Exciting Quilts Using Block Blends

Blends

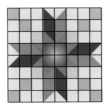

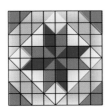

**Stepping Stones
and Framed Star**

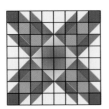

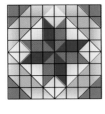

**Woven Star and
Framed Star**

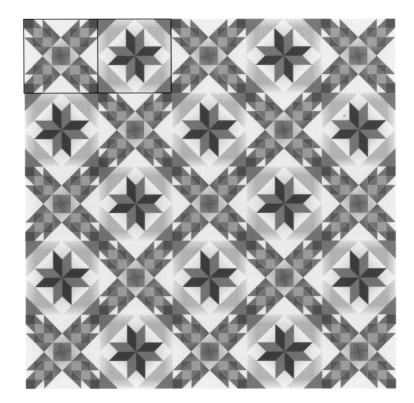

Intriguing Nine-Patch Pattern Blends

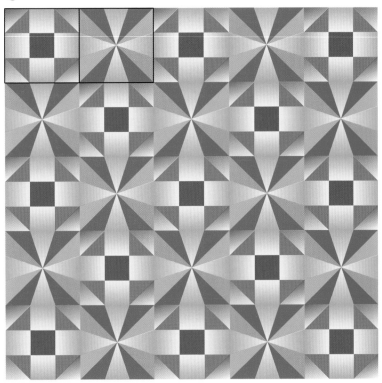

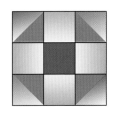

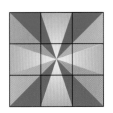

Shoofly and Gift Box

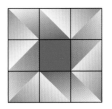

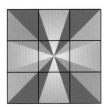

Formal Garden
and Gift Box

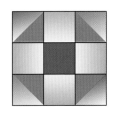

Exciting Quilts Using Block Blends

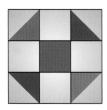

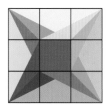

Shoofly and
Spinning Around
the Block

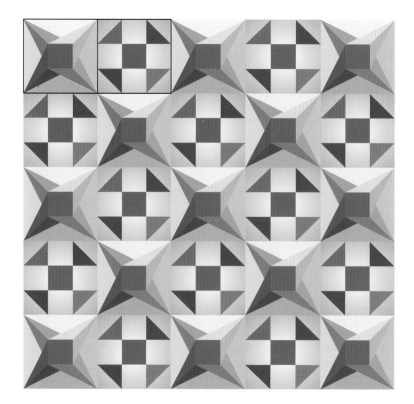

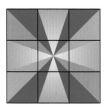

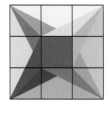

Gift Box and
Spinning Around
the Block

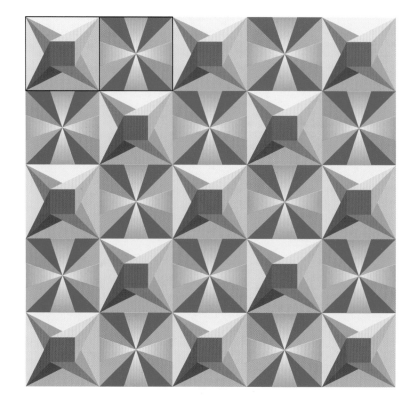

Make Any Block Any Size

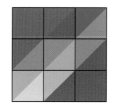

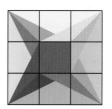

Northwind and Spinning Around the Block: Traditional Setting

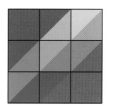

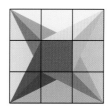

Northwind: Rotated One-Quarter Turn and Spinning Around the Block

Exciting Quilts Using Block Blends

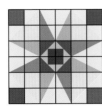

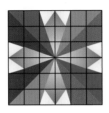

Storm at Sea and
Diamond in the
Rough

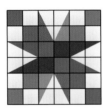

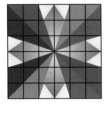

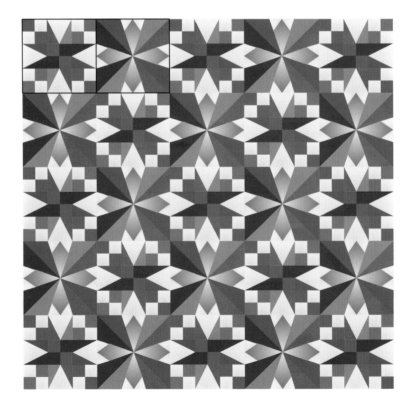

Fifty-four-Forty or
Fight and Diamond
in the Rough

Make Any Block Any Size

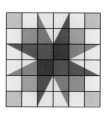

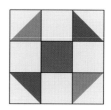

Shoofly and Fifty-four-Forty or Fight

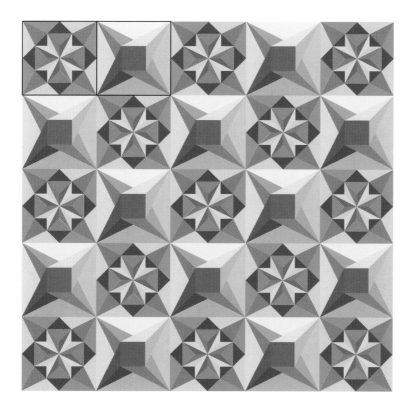

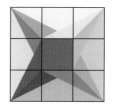

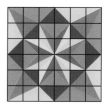

Spinning Around the Block and Wedding Ring Glow

Exciting Quilts Using Block Blends

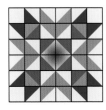

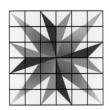

Wyoming Valley
and Dancing Star

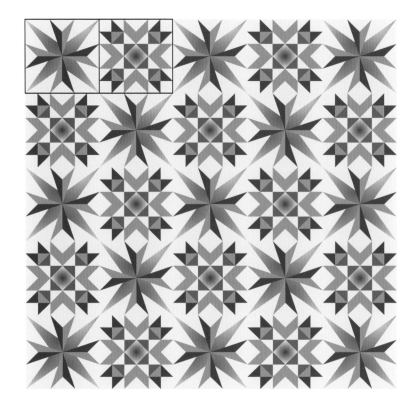

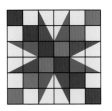

Fifty-four-Forty or
Fight and Dancing
Star

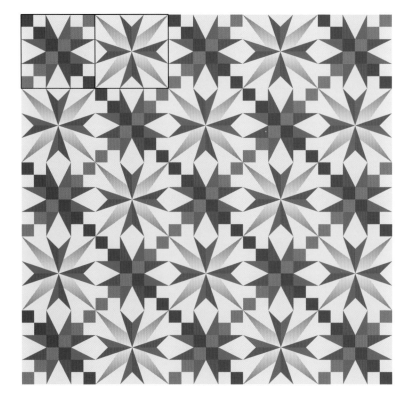

Make Any Block Any Size

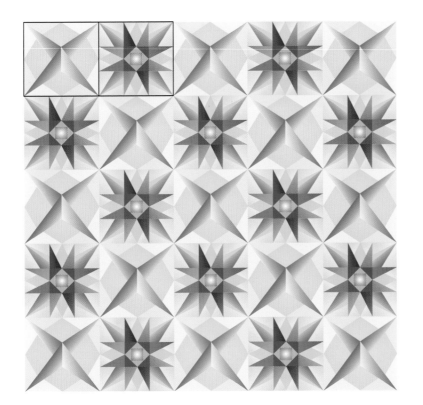

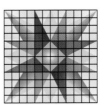

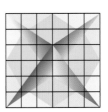

Star Echoes and
Star Walk

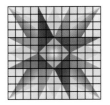

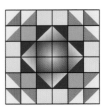

Summer Winds and
Star Echoes

Exciting Quilts Using Block Blends

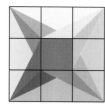

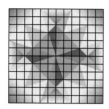

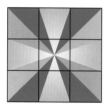

Spinning Around
the Block and
Vermont

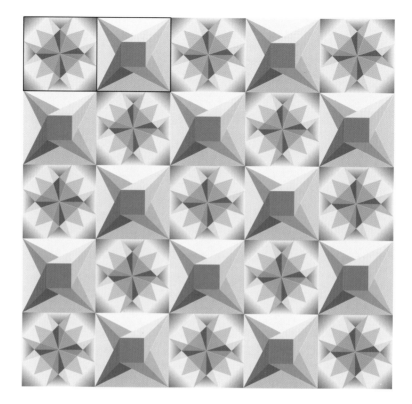

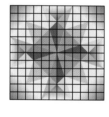

Gift Box
and Vermont

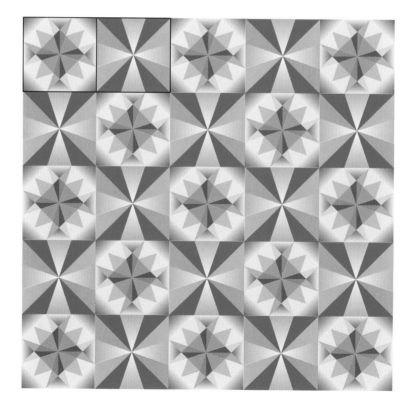

Make Any Block Any Size

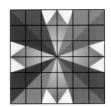

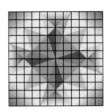

Diamond in the
Rough and Vermont

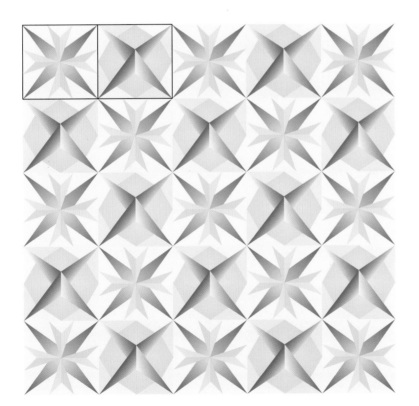

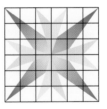

Star Walk and
Dancing Star

Exciting Quilts Using Block Blends

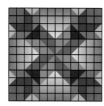

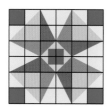

Storm at Sea and
Blazing Star

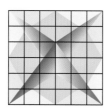

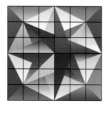

Star Walk and
Puzzling Star

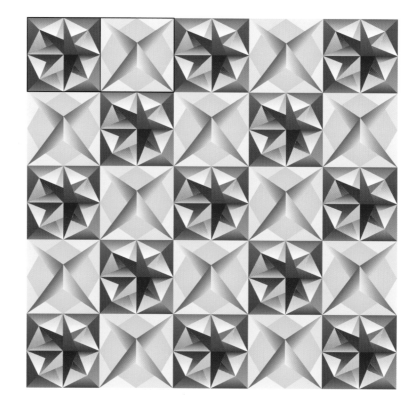

Blends

Make Any Block Any Size

Captivating Five-Patch Pattern Blends

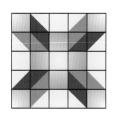

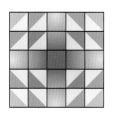

Farmer's Daughter
and Flying Geese

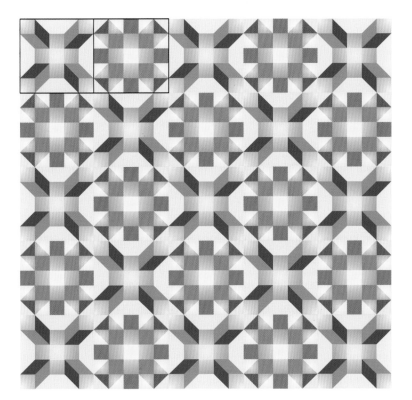

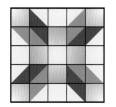

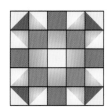

Farmer's Daughter
and Sister's Choice

Exciting Quilts Using Block Blends

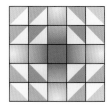

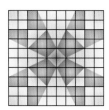

Flying Geese and
Dutch Mill

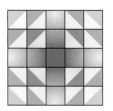

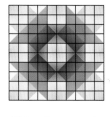

Flying Geese and
Golden Royalty

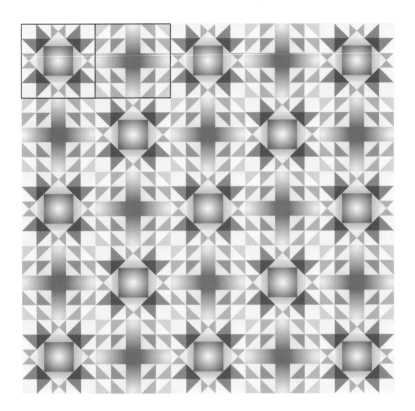

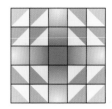

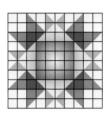

Flying Geese and
King David's Crown

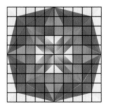

Bachelor's Puzzle
and Starry
Roundabout

Exciting Quilts Using Block Blends

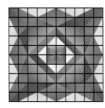

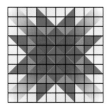

Poinsettia in
Bloom and
Mexican Cross

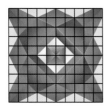

Poinsettia in
Bloom and Churn
Dash

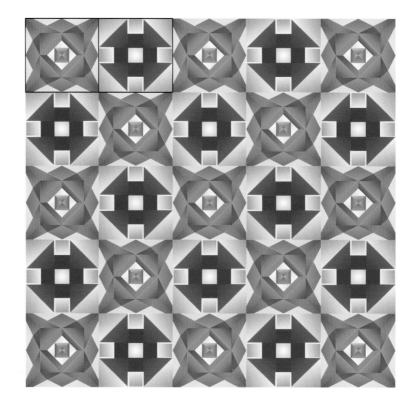

Make Any Block Any Size

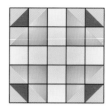

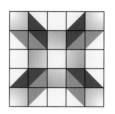

Duck and Ducklings
and Farmer's
Daughter

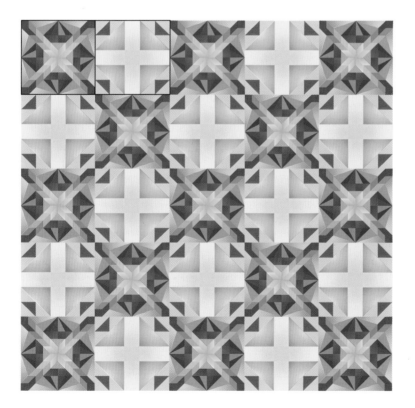

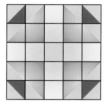

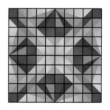

Duck and Ducklings
and Glowing Stars
and Gems

Exciting Quilts Using Block Blends

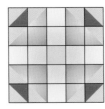

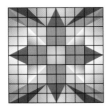

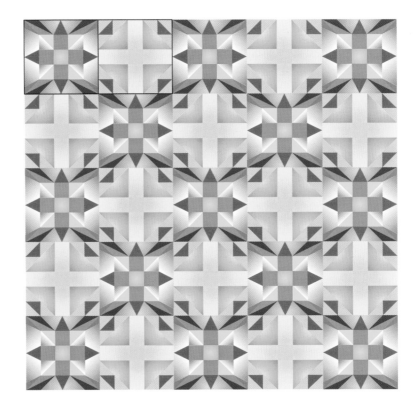

Duck and
Ducklings and
Imaginary Curves

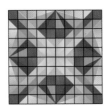

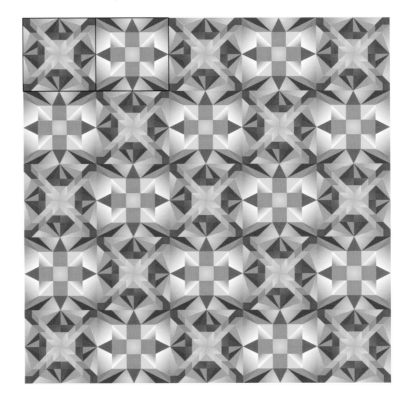

Glowing Stars and
Gems and
Imaginary Curves

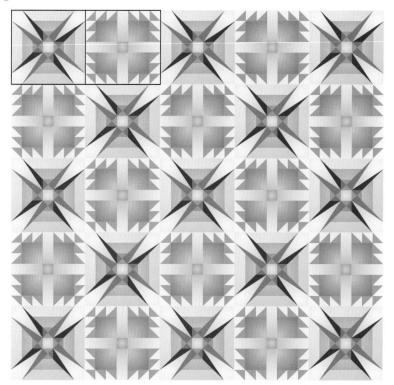

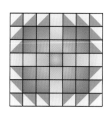

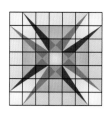

Hen and Chickens
and Star Stretch

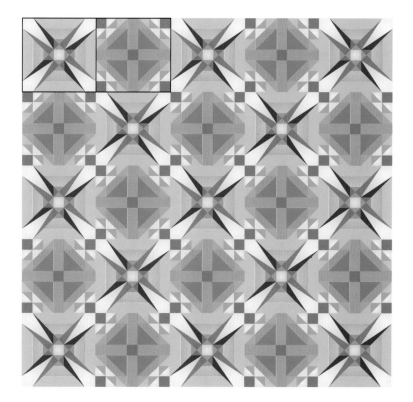

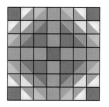

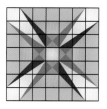

Dove in the Window
and Star Stretch

Blends

131   Exciting Quilts Using Block Blends

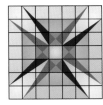

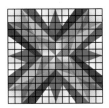

Star Stretch and
Hidden Star

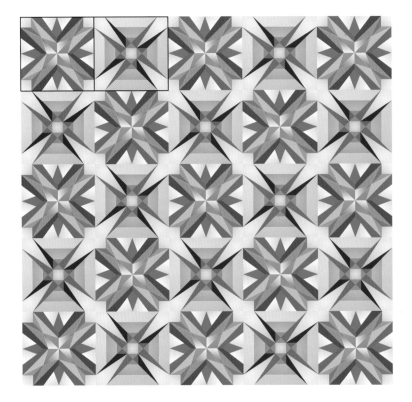

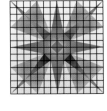

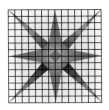

Star Trek and
Peacock Dance

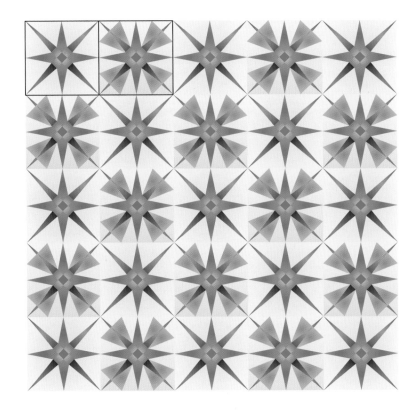

Make Any Block Any Size

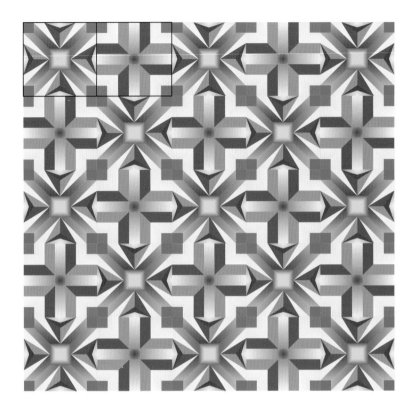

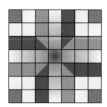

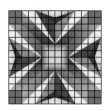

Stone Mason's
Puzzle and Through
the Looking Glass

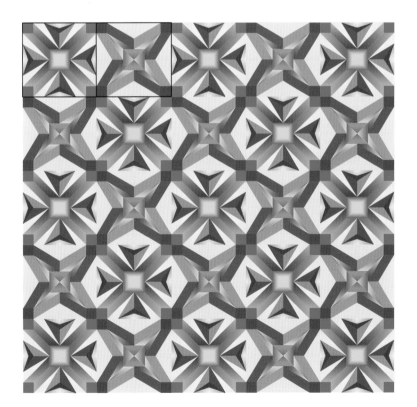

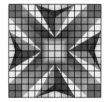

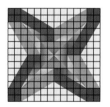

Through the Looking
Glass and Diamond
Weave

Exciting Quilts Using Block Blends

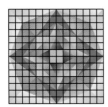

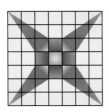

Star Trek and
Australian
Gemstone

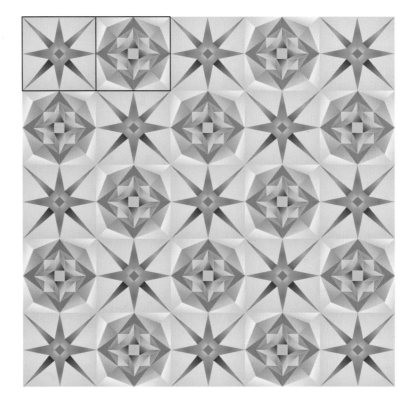

Star Light, Star
Bright and Star
Burst

Make Any Block Any Size

Activities and Extended Learning

Project Ideas

New concepts are learned best with small projects, which give you success and joy. For this reason, I suggest working with small quilts for most projects. Once learned, new ideas can be incorporated easily into larger, more difficult projects.

Small projects can include beautiful lap quilts, which can be a welcome gift for family members or special friends. They can be used while reading a book, watching television, or taking a mid-day nap. Wall quilts are also good projects, as are miniature quilts for the wall, doll bed, or doll house.

In addition, you may wish to donate these small quilt projects to worthwhile causes. There are many options from which to choose. Small lap quilts are perfect gifts for children in hospitals, battered-women's shelters, or foster care. People in homeless shelters, teenagers in juvenile centers, or elderly people in convalescent centers or nursing homes could also use these small quilts. There are so many people who would love to wrap themselves in a quilt, which gives them warmth in both body and spirit. Doll quilts (with a doll) make very special gifts for children benefiting from Christmas charity organizations. Also, your projects may be welcome additions to your favorite organization's fundraising auction.

Activities For Four-Patch Patterns (Chapter Two)

1. Choose a pattern from each of the four-patch pattern family groups: basic, simple, and complex. Place the basic four-patch pattern in a 7" square. Place the simple four-patch pattern in an $11\frac{1}{2}$" square. Make a 14" square for the complex pattern drawing. After you have drawn the three different patterns, consider using at least one of them for a small project.

2. Choose a four-patch pattern to use as the design for a potholder. Determine your potholder's size—thus your block's size. Draw the square, its grid lines, and the pattern, using the instructions provided on pages 15-16, 20-21, 24-26, or 29-31. Make your templates or prepare for your paper-piecing foundation. Choose the fabrics. Begin construction.

   Patchwork potholders are far superior to commercial potholders when cotton batting is used. I cut up old, thick cotton bath towels to use as batting. Often I put the towel batting between two layers of cotton flannel (like a sandwich). If the towel is thin, I double the towel layer. Cotton toweling and flannel is more effective than polyester batting. Polyester conducts heat too readily to be satisfactory.

3. Select one of your favorite 16-square grid designs to make a lap quilt. Make certain you like its overall design when it's placed in a multiple-block setting. Determine what size quilt you wish to make and what size block you will use. Draw the pattern, using the instructions on pages 24-26. Make templates or prepare for foundation piecing. Choose fabrics. Begin your quilt's construction.

4. Make a quilt for a particular bed in your home. First, choose a favorite 64-square grid four-patch pattern that is especially pleasing in an overall design. Select a favorite season (or color scale) to use as a color guide for this quilt. Decide the best block size to use in this quilt. Draw the block, using the instructions on pages 29-31. Make the templates or prepare for your favorite paper-piecing foundation method. Choose fabrics. Construct your project in your usual manner.

5. If you want to make your own original pattern design, first draw a small square (e.g. 2" or 4"). Place a 64-square grid in this square. Choose any four-patch pattern to use as a beginning point for creating your own pattern. Lightly draw this pattern in your square. Begin adding and subtracting lines to create your own pattern, using the grid lines to help you. After you are satisfied with your results, make several copies of the block. Cut them out, so you can place them together into an overall quilt design. Make additional changes, if needed. For instance, you may want to add more lines or erase a line that isn't visually pleasing.

Once you are pleased with your original design, decide what project you would like to make. Determine the best block size. Draw the block. Make templates or prepare for paper piecing. Select fabrics. Construct your quilt in your usual manner.

Activities For Nine-Patch Patterns (Chapter Three)

1. Choose a pattern from each of the nine-patch pattern family groups: basic, simple, and complex. Next, draw each selected pattern in the following block sizes: Place the basic nine-patch pattern (three equal divisions) in a 5" square. Place the simple nine-patch pattern (six equal divisions) in a 10" square. Place the complex nine-patch pattern (twelve equal divisions) in a 13½" square. After you have drawn the three different patterns, choose one of these for a small project.

2. Select a nine-patch pattern. Draw the pattern in a 3" block. Make templates or create a paper-piecing foundation. Create a baby quilt or doll quilt with this pattern.

3. Draw a simple nine-patch pattern, using the instructions on pages 44-46. Design a summer spread (a picnic cloth) using this block pattern.

4. Select a complex nine-patch block pattern to use for a small quilt. Draw the pattern using the instructions on pages 47-49 or make your paper-piecing foundation. Select the fabrics and construct your project.

5. Create your own block pattern by first drawing a small square (e.g. 3"). Using the instructions on page 47-49, draw grid lines for a complex pattern. Once you have the grid lines drawn, choose a pattern to use as a beginning point. Lightly draw this pattern's lines on your grid. Study the pattern. Begin adding and subtracting lines to create your own pattern. Once you are pleased with your new design, make copies of it. Cut out the patterns and make a paper-quilt design. If you need to change some lines in your original block, do so now.

Once you are satisfied with the overall design, decide on the type of quilt you will make with your new design. Determine the quilt's size and the block size. Draw the block pattern to that size. Make templates or prepare for paper piecing. Choose the fabrics. Construct the quilt in your preferred manner.

Activities For Five-Patch Patterns (Chapter Four)

1. Select a pattern from both of the five-patch pattern family groups: simple and complex (five and ten equal divisions). Draw each selected pattern in the following block size: Place the simple five-patch pattern (five equal divisions) in a 7¾" square. Place the complex five-patch pattern (ten equal divisions) in an 11½" square. Save these two patterns for future projects.

2. Select a simple five-patch block to use for a doll quilt or miniature quilt. Use a block that is no more than 4" square. Draw the square; next draw the block's grid lines and pattern. Choose the fabrics. Construct the quilt.

3. Using a complex five-patch pattern, design a small medallion quilt. Select a block that will give enough interest and support to provide a beautiful central motif. For the surrounding borders, use many of the shapes introduced in the central area. You may use these shapes in a wide variety of combinations. For good design control, plan to have each side border no wider than half the measurement of the central design area. For in-depth information about borders, see pages 127-129 in *The Visual Dance* (see Suggested Resource Books).

To create your own pattern, begin by drawing a 4" square. Using the instructions on pages 77-81, draw grid lines for a complex pattern. Once you have the grid lines drawn, choose a pattern to use as a beginning point. Lightly draw the pattern's lines on your grid. Study the pattern. Then begin adding and subtracting lines from the pattern. As you work, a new design should evolve.

Once you are pleased with your new design, make copies of it. Cut out the patterns and put them together in a paper quilt. Observe how well the blocks work in a multiple-block setting. Make any necessary changes. Create a quilt of your choice, using your original design.

Activities For Seven-Patch Patterns (Chapter Five)

1. Select a pattern from both of the seven-patch pattern family groups: simple and complex (seven and fourteen equal divisions). Draw each selected pattern in the following block size: Place the simple seven-patch pattern (seven equal divisions) in a 4½" square. Place the complex seven-patch pattern (fourteen equal divisions) in a 12" square. Save these two patterns for future projects.

2. Choose one of your favorite simple seven-patch patterns to create a lap quilt. Determine the block size. Draw the square, its grid lines, and the pattern. Select fabrics for the foreground design that are bold and exciting. Construct the quilt.

3. Select a complex seven-patch pattern to use for planning and creating a medallion wall quilt. Determine the quilt size, the quilt's configuration (e.g. square, vertical rectangle, horizontal rectangle), and the block size. Then plan the quilt's center. After the center area has been designed, determine the width and design of each border.

A visually successful design works best when a side's total border width is no wider than half the width of the center area. Therefore, if your central design is 36" wide, your quilt's total border sides should be 18" or less in either direction. If you need a larger quilt, begin by making the center area larger to accommodate a wider border. Remember, a border's primary function is to provide closure, and support or reiterate elements in the body of the quilt. No new ideas should be presented in a border, as they will distract from the quilt's primary design. For detailed information about borders see *The Visual Dance*, pages 127-129. A less detailed border summary may be found in *Patchwork Persuasion*, pages 25-27.

When you are pleased with your overall design, begin drawing the design for the center area of your quilt. Make the templates or prepare your paper-piecing foundation. Pick the fabrics. Begin construction.

Activities For Enticing Patterns for Special Quilts (Chapter Six)

1. If you have a favorite young boy in your life, design your own sailboat quilt. You can use either Sailboats or Sailing Away (page 98), one of your own designs, or a combination of patterns. Draw the patterns. Prepare templates or paper piecing. Choose your fabrics. Begin construction.

2. Create your own house quilt by using the pattern Back Home (pages 99-100) as your guide. Change the pattern as much as you wish. Use fillers in a spontaneous manner. If you want to add details, such as trees, bushes, flowers, and birds, consider mixing techniques by using appliqué or stitchery for these extra highlights.

3. Design a spring or summer bed quilt, using one of the flower designs (Spring Anemone, Blooming Poppy II, Climbing Nasturtium, and Trumpeter's Glory, pages 101-102). You may use the patterns exactly as they are drawn, or you may make changes to fit your needs.

4. Design an autumn quilt, using either Maple Leaf or Autumn Days (page 103) as your pattern. Use as many different autumnal fabrics as possible to make this a dynamic quilt. Also, consider using fillers to allow the leaves to randomly float throughout your quilt.

5. Create a winter holiday bed or lap quilt using the pattern Star Wreath (page 104). When choosing colors for your quilt, make certain one color family is dominant, another is secondary, and any other color families included are used as accents.

6. Create a wall quilt for the winter holidays by using the pattern Candles of Joy (page 105). The block background will be pieced; the candles and flames will be appliquéd. Determine the block size. Begin designing your quilt. Draw the pieced block. Make the patterns for the candles and flames. After you have done the preliminary work, begin construction.

Activities For Block Blends (Chapter Seven)

1. Look at the illustrated quilts using four-patch pattern blends on pages 106-114. Choose your favorite blend. Draw the patterns in your preferred size. Create a lap or bed quilt with this blend. Try to incorporate as many fabrics as possible for each color family shown in the illustration. This will create a richer, more dynamic quilt than if you simply use one fabric for each pattern piece.

2. Observe the illustrated quilts on pages 115-124, which are made from nine-patch pattern blends. Select one for a wall quilt. Determine the block and quilt size. Design the quilt. Draw the patterns. Select the colors and fabrics for your quilt. Use as many fabrics as you can within each color family. Construct the quilt.

3. Look at the five-patch pattern blends shown on pages 125-130. Choose your favorite combination to create a bed quilt. Plan your quilt's design by determining the blocks' size, the colors, and the fabrics. Draw both patterns. Determine your method of piecing. Begin construction.

4. Study the illustrated quilts using seven-patch pattern blends (pages 131-134). Choose your favorite blend to create a small quilt for a special friend or family member. Design a wall quilt using this blend. Determine the blocks' size. Draw the pattern. Prepare templates or paper piecing. Begin construction.

6. Study the different patch-pattern blocks shown in the previous chapters. Select two blocks from one patch-pattern family to blend for a project of your choice. Make small paper-block samples. Then make several paper copies of each block. Play with the design. If you are pleased with the overall blended design, begin working on your project by drawing your patterns. If your design does not please you, make another selection. Make certain the combination is one you are excited about making. Create this quilt using your favorite color as the dominant hue.

Bibliography

Beyer, Jinny. *The Quilter's Album of Blocks & Borders.* McLean, Virginia: EPM Publications, Inc., 1980.

Brackman, Barbara, comp. *Encyclopedia of Pieced Quilt Patterns.* Paducah, Kentucky: American Quilter's Society, 1993.

Mills, Susan Winter. *849 Traditional Patchwork Patterns.* New York, New York: Dover Publications, Inc., 1989.

Malone, Maggie. *1,001 Patchwork Designs.* New York, New York: Sterling Publishing Co., Inc. 1982.

Wolfrom, Joen. *Patchwork Persuasion.* Lafayette, California: C&T Publishing, 1997.

Wolfrom, Joen. *The Visual Dance: Creating Spectacular Quilts.* Lafayette, California: C&T Publishing, 1995.

Suggested Resource Books

An Amish Adventure by Roberta Horton

Appliqué 12 Easy Ways! by Elly Sienkiewicz

Easy Paper-Pieced Keepsake Quilts by Carol Doak

Firm Foundations by Jane Hall and Dixie Hayward

Heirloom Machine Quilting by Harriet Hargrave

The Magical Effects of Color by Joen Wolfrom (out of print)

Patchwork Quilts Made Easy by Jean Wells

Patchwork Persuasion by Joen Wolfrom

Plaids & Stripes by Roberta Horton

Quilts for Fabric Lovers by Alex Anderson

Quilts, Quilts, and More Quilts! by Diana McClun and Laura Nownes

Say It With Quilts by Diana McClun and Laura Nownes

Simply Stars by Alex Anderson

Small Scale Quiltmaking by Sally Collins

Start Quilting by Alex Anderson

Tradition with a Twist by Blanche Young and Dalene Young Stone

The Visual Dance by Joen Wolfrom

Quilters'® Newsletter Magazine, Post Office Box 394, Wheatridge, Colorado 80033

PATTERN INDEX

Pattern Index

SUBJECT INDEX

About the Author

Joen began quiltmaking in 1974 after she left her career in education to become a homemaker. Her interest in color, design, and contemporary quilt art surfaced in the early 1980s. During that time, Joen challenged herself to experiment with new techniques and visual ideas. She is noted for being the innovator of several techniques, including strip-pieced landscapes and organic curved designs (curves on the whole). She was the innovator of the free-form freezer paper technique, which is often used in curved and straight-line piecing. Her work is included in collections throughout the world.

Joen has taught and lectured in the quilting field both nationally and internationally since 1984. Additionally, she is frequently invited to jury and judge international, national, and regional shows. Her previously published books are *Patchwork Persuasion: Fascinating Quilts from Traditional Designs*; *The Visual Dance*; *The Magical Effects of Color*; and *Landscapes & Illusions: Creating Scenic Imagery with Fabric*.

Joen's other interests include gardening and landscape design, playing bridge, reading, and spending quiet times with friends and family. When not traveling, Joen enjoys the private quietness of her family's home in the rural setting of a small island in Washington State. There she enjoys life with her three children and husband—Danielle, Dane, David, and Dan.

Inquiries about workshop and lecture bookings and other correspondence may be sent directly to Joen Wolfrom at 104 Bon Bluff, Fox Island, Washington 98333. Requests for a current teaching schedule may be sent to the same address (include a large self-addressed, stamped envelope). Her home page may be visited at www.mplx.com/joenwolfrom.

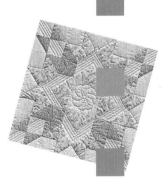

Other Fine Books From C&T Publishing:

An Amish Adventure, 2nd Edition,
Roberta Horton

Anatomy of a Doll, The Fabric Sculptor's Handbook, Susanna Oroyan

Appliqué 12 Easy Ways! Elly Sienkiewicz

Art & Inspirations, Ruth B. McDowell,
Ruth B. McDowell

The Art of Silk Ribbon Embroidery,
Judith Baker Montano

The Artful Ribbon, Candace Kling

At Home with Patrick Lose, Colorful Quilted Projects, Patrick Lose

Baltimore Album Legacy, Catalog of C&T Publishing's 1998 Baltimore Album Quilt Show and Contest,
Elly Sienkiewicz

Baltimore Beauties and Beyond (Volume I), Elly Sienkiewicz

Basic Seminole Patchwork,
Cheryl Greider Bradkin

A Colorful Book, Yvonne Porcella

Colors Changing Hue, Yvonne Porcella

Crazy Quilt Handbook, Judith Montano

Crazy Quilt Odyssey, Judith Montano

Crazy with Cotton, Diana Leone

Curves in Motion, Quilt Designs & Techniques, Judy B. Dales

Deidre Scherer, Work in Fabric and Thread, Deidre Scherer

Designing the Doll, From Concept to Construction, Susanna Oroyan

Easy Pieces, Creative Color Play with Two Simple Quilt Blocks, Margaret Miller

Elegant Stitches, An Illustrated Stitch Guide & Source Book of Inspiration, Judith Baker Montano

Everything Flowers, Quilts from the Garden, Jean and Valori Wells

The Fabric Makes the Quilt,
Roberta Horton

Fantastic Figures, Ideas & Techniques Using the New Clays,
Susanna Oroyan

Focus on Features, Life-like Portrayals in Appliqué, Charlotte Warr Andersen

Forever Yours, Wedding Quilts, Clothing & Keepsakes, Amy Barickman

Fractured Landscape Quilts,
Katie Pasquini Masopust

Free Stuff for Quilters on the Internet,
Judy Heim and Gloria Hansen

From Fiber to Fabric, The Essential Guide to Quiltmaking Textiles,
Harriet Hargrave

Hand Quilting with Alex Anderson, Six Projects for Hand Quilters,
Alex Anderson

Heirloom Machine Quilting, Third Edition, Harriet Hargrave

Imagery on Fabric, Second Edition,
Jean Ray Laury

Impressionist Palette, Gai Perry

Impressionist Quilts, Gai Perry

Jacobean Rhapsodies, Composing with 28 Appliqué Designs,
Patricia Campbell and Mimi Ayers

Judith B. Montano, Art & Inspirations,
Judith B. Montano

Kaleidoscopes, Wonders of Wonder,
Cozy Baker

Kaleidoscopes & Quilts, Paula Nadelstern

Mariner's Compass Quilts, New Directions, Judy Mathieson

Mastering Machine Appliqué,
Harriet Hargrave

Michael James, Art & Inspirations,
Michael James

The New Sampler Quilt, Diana Leone

On the Surface, Thread Embellishment & Fabric Manipulation, Wendy Hill

Papercuts and Plenty, Vol. III of Baltimore Beauties and Beyond,
Elly Sienkiewicz

The Photo Transfer Handbook, Snap It, Print It, Stitch It! Jean Ray Laury

Piecing, Expanding the Basics,
Ruth B. McDowell

Plaids & Stripes, The Use of Directional Fabrics in Quilts, Roberta Horton

Quilts for Fabric Lovers, Alex Anderson

Quilts from the Civil War, Nine Projects, Historical Notes, Diary Entries,
Barbara Brackman

Quilts, Quilts, and More Quilts!
Diana McClun and Laura Nownes

RIVA, If Ya Wanna Look Good, Honey, Your Feet Gotta Hurt...,
Ruth Reynolds

Rotary Cutting with Alex Anderson, Tips • Techniques • Projects,
Alex Anderson

Say It with Quilts, Diana McClun and Laura Nownes

Scrap Quilts, The Art of Making Do,
Roberta Horton

Simply Stars, Quilts that Sparkle,
Alex Anderson

Six Color World, Color, Cloth, Quilts & Wearables, Yvonne Porcella

Soft-Edge Piecing, Jinny Beyer

Start Quilting with Alex Anderson, Six Projects for First-Time Quilters,
Alex Anderson

Stripes in Quilts, Mary Mashuta

Through the Garden Gate, Quilters and Their Gardens,
Jean and Valori Wells

Tradition with a Twist, Variations on Your Favorite Quilts, Blanche Young and Dalene Young Stone

Trapunto by Machine, Hari Walner

Wildflowers, Designs for Appliqué and Quilting, Carol Armstrong

Yvonne Porcella, Art & Inspirations,
Yvonne Porcella

For more information write
for a free catalog from:
C&T Publishing, Inc.
P.O. Box 1456
Lafayette, CA 94549
(800) 284-1114
www.ctpub.com
e-mail: ctinfo@ctpub.com

For quilting supplies:
Cotton Patch Mail Order
3405 Hall Lane, Dept. CTB
Lafayette, CA 94549
www.quiltusa.com
e-mail: quiltusa@yahoo.com
(800) 835-4418
(925) 283-7883